InfoQuest:

A New Twist on Information Literacy

Peggy S. Milam

Linworth
PUBLISHING, INC.

Linworth Publishing, Inc.
Worthington, Ohio

Cataloging-in-Publication Data

Milam, Peggy S., 1953-
     InfoQuest: a new twist on information literacy / by Peggy S. Milam.
          p. cm.
     Includes bibliographical references and index.
     ISBN 1-58683-022-8
Information literacy—Study and teaching—Activity programs—United States. 2.
     School libraries—Activity programs—United States. I. Title

ZA3075 .M55 2001
027.8'222'0973—dc21   2001038552

Published by Linworth Publishing, Inc.
480 East Wilson Bridge Road, Suite L
Worthington, Ohio 43085

Copyright © 2002 by Linworth Publishing Incorporated

ISBN 1-58683-022-8

5 4 3 2 1

About the Author

Peggy Milam is a certified Library Media Specialist with more than 25 years of teaching experience in both public and private schools in the state of Georgia. She has previously published articles in *Capers for Kids*, *Atlanta Parent* and *Library Talk*, as well as co-authored a book, *Kids' Atlanta*. Peggy has presented InfoQuest at the Conference on Children's Literature in Athens, Georgia and the Georgia Independent School Conference in Atlanta.

Dedication

For my eleventh grade English teacher, Barbara Reed, who taught me not to be too "wordy," for Kat and Gretchen, dear friends who encouraged me, for my children, Ryan and Kristen, who have been my inspiration always, and in honor of J.C., my guiding light.

Table of Contents

Table of Contents *continued*

Table of Contents continued

Table of Contents continued

Table of Contents *continued*

Table of Contents *continued*

List of Figures

Introduction

How InfoQuest Began

Mount Vernon Presbyterian School is a private school in north Atlanta, Georgia that serves grades PS-8. It has an outstanding faculty, supportive parents, a low student-teacher ratio, and high-achieving students. Sounds idyllic, right? It is in many respects, but recently the school had one serious problem.

The problem was the school library media center. It was located in a long, narrow room. Circling the walls were musty bookshelves creaking under the load of too many books in too little space. Mount Vernon desperately needed to give the media center an overhaul, and it did. The center was moved to a wider, lighter room. Bright new shelves were built and a woodsy wall mural was painted in the story corner. A new computer workstation was outfitted with networked Macintosh computers. It was a cheery, inviting atmosphere, all ready for the students to visit. But they didn't. Outside of the dutifully scheduled classes, students rarely came in at all.

Being left alone in the media center gave me time to ponder the situation, to wonder, and to dream. Obviously, we needed more than a facelift to attract the students. We needed a magnet! I thought, what if the media center was a fun place to visit? What if gathering information was a sort of game, with prizes? What if we made up challenging questions and encouraged the students to come on their own to find the answers? Bingo! InfoQuest was born.

InfoQuest is a game of challenging research questions that can be answered in the school library media center. Each week a different question is posed on the intercom and students have all week to come to the media center to research the answer. Younger children are given hints and much more guidance, but all ages are encouraged to participate. Prizes are distributed on Friday for the students who have found the correct answer.

If a student is out of school when the question of the week is announced, each teacher can supply the question from his/her own master list. Additionally, a flip chart of questions is kept in the media center in a central location clipped open to the question of the week. (Questions are asked at random, so no one knows what the next question will be.) Students must come to the media center to answer the question, and even if they have found out the answer from another source, they must verify the answer in the resources we have available. Questions vary from week to week as do the resources used to locate the answer. By the end of the school year, students who have been regular participants will have used nearly every type of print or nonprint resource available.

Response to the program has been tremendous. Parents became excited by the interest their children were showing in the program, and, from the onset, they pledged $16,500 to purchase 1,000 new books for research. This pledge tripled our yearly funding. With the curiosity piqued by the weekly questions and the exciting new books in our collection to choose from, children were even more eager to check out books. Our weekly circulation doubled. Teachers rushed in to try to find out the InfoQuest answers ahead of their students, and many stayed and browsed the periodicals or checked out supplemental materials. Twenty-five percent more teachers became active patrons. Parental volunteers went from zero to six regulars as parents became intrigued with the new program and volunteered to help out. Most importantly, student research skills became the focus of our new program beginning in the first grade. All of these improvements are a direct result of our InfoQuest program and simultaneously worked to build influence for the school library media center. In a nutshell, our influence grew from a game:

- We set a Goal to improve patronage
- We Appealed to all ages
- We Motivated patrons to continue coming
- We Excited the administration, parents, and teachers who support it.

InfoQuest: A New Twist on Information Literacy is a comprehensive guide to implementing the InfoQuest program in other libraries, schools, and school library media centers across the country. Based on the original article published in the Jan/Feb 1999 issue of *Library Talk* Magazine, the book details the state of information literacy, the need for instructing students in information literacy, a continuum of skills, ideas for collaboration between classroom teachers and school library media specialists, how metacognition relates to framing good research questions, a how-to guide for program development, plus all the questions and answers a practitioner might need to keep the program going for years.

The book is intended to attract teachers, school library media specialists, public librarians and program directors, school administrators, school boards, parents (especially home-schoolers), instructors in teacher preparation and instructional technology programs, and any others interested in innovative ideas for education and library services.

InfoQuest presents a unique approach to the teaching of information literacy skills. The program is easy to implement and is delineated into groups of information literacy skills at varying levels from preliminary researchers to advanced. Research questions are provided in a variety of subject areas and at all levels. No other information literacy program is as detailed and comprehensive in scope.

The book is practical and based on a tried-and-true format with a proven success record. Everything a practitioner might need to fully and successfully implement the program is included, along with resources for individualizing the program. Included are assessment tools, ideas for fund-raising and a comprehensive skills continuum that simplifies lesson planning at all levels.

The book is arranged in three parts: Perspective, Philosophy, Practice. The Perspective section deals with what information literacy is, why it should be taught, and the current state of information literacy in education. The Philosophy section describes the how-tos: how to teach information literacy more effectively, how to ask higher-order questions, and how to teach InfoQuest itself. The Practice section provides questions and answers by subject and level as well as assessment tools for tracking the progress of the participants. Each chapter in the Practice section contains additional references for individualizing InfoQuest programs and the book includes a name and subject index.

Chapter 1

What is Information Literacy?

Over the past decade, unprecedented growth in technology and Internet access has caused our society to become information-powered. With the advent of computer databases, networking, and other technological innovations that facilitate information retrieval, information storage has been compounded at an incredible rate. Consider the following statistics:

> **"Information overload costs businesses and individuals valuable time, effort and additional resources... and the cost is rising"**
>
> *— Mark Nelson, 2000, p 1.*

■ More new information has been produced in the past 30 years than in the last five millennia (Nelson, 2000, p. 3).

■ More than one million books are published annually with an additional 100,000 printed by the U.S. Government alone (Kranich, 2000, p. 5).

■ More than three decades ago, 20 million words of technological data were recorded every 24 hours (Murray, 1966, p. 3).

■ Over three billion web pages are available on the World Wide Web and the number is growing by 5 million new pages a day (Kranich, p. 5).

Is it any wonder that this era has been dubbed the Information Age?

Characteristics of the Information Age

> **"Information drives the education field, the media, consulting and service companies, postal services, lawyers, accountants, writers, certain government employees, as well as those in data communications and storage"**
>
> — *Richard Saul Wurman, 1989, p. 39.*

For those of us whose employment revolves around information retrieval and disbursement, these statistics are both encouraging and alarming. Over a decade ago, Wurman (1989) noted that "…a weekday edition of the *New York Times* contains more information than the average person was likely to come across in a lifetime in 17th Century England" (p. 32).

The availability of more information than ever before in history means that more skills are required than ever before to select what information is necessary, whether it be for home or for business. Today the flow of information is so great that no aspect of life remains untouched by it, whether it is personal or professional.

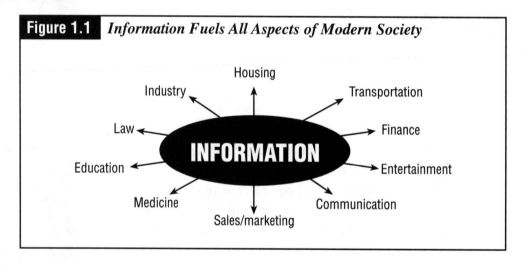

Figure 1.1 *Information Fuels All Aspects of Modern Society*

Quick and accurate access to information fuels government, medicine, business, entertainment—virtually every segment of our society. Rarely does a business operate profitably without the need for corporate research to stay ahead of the competition and become informed of the forces behind the current rate of supply and demand. In fact, every business day, lack of information can cost corporations many thousands of dollars in product development, market analysis, investments and expenditures, insurance, employee safety and benefits, and litigation prevention.

Information Literacy Skills in the Workplace

In order to be prepared to enter this rapidly transforming workplace, today's students must learn to retrieve, organize, and communicate more information than ever before. A working knowledge of this process has been dubbed "information literacy."

Consider the difference between workers during the Industrial Revolution and workers during the Information Revolution. During the Industrial Revolution, skilled labor was the norm. Workers were often apprenticed to learn a trade, which was generally practiced for a lifetime. Labor was more often physical than mental. Job mobility was less common and workers were employed to perform a single task, often in a factory or an assembly line. Rarely were workers re-educated to become more skilled or to advance. Information was generated by industry itself.

> "Economic and social change is generating new demands for lifelong learning that will not be satisfied in terms of quantity, quality or convenience by traditional attendance programs"
>
> *— Higher Education Council, 1997, p. 5.*

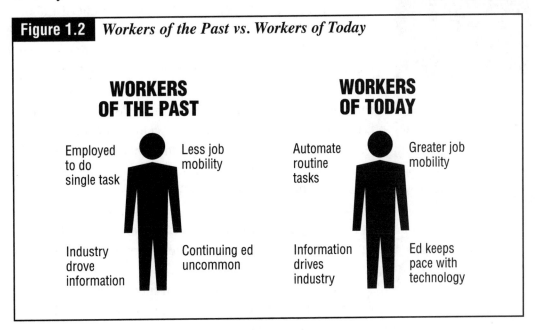

Figure 1.2 *Workers of the Past vs. Workers of Today*

WORKERS OF THE PAST

Employed to do single task

Less job mobility

Industry drove information

Continuing ed uncommon

WORKERS OF TODAY

Automate routine tasks

Greater job mobility

Information drives industry

Ed keeps pace with technology

Workers in the Information Revolution, on the other hand, expect to be upwardly mobile in their jobs. Rarely does an employee work at one job for a lifetime and may even change careers several times. Labor is more often mental than physical. Continuing education is common, even expected of employees. Lifelong learning is the buzzword in the educational arena and beyond, and information literacy skills are a necessity, as information drives industry.

This age of information has produced such a barrage of data that expertise in searching and sorting information is necessary for both individuals and businesses to compete in an international market. Will today's students be prepared for competition in the workforce? Will current information literacy programs be sufficient to meet future needs?

As we ponder these and other questions about preparedness for the future, it is important to understand what experts are telling educators about information literacy.

Expert Definitions of Information Literacy

> "The demand for electronically mediated resource-based learning programs will grow exponentially over the next decade with the rapid development of technology and changes to workforce environment"
>
> — *Higher Education Council, 1997, p. 5.*

Many groups associated with education and job training have attempted to define information literacy. The Southern Association of Colleges and Schools (1996), defines information literacy as the "ability to locate, evaluate, and use information to become independent life-long learners" (p.1). The State University of New York Council of Library Directors in its Information Literacy Initiative (1997) defines information literacy as "the abilities to recognize when information is needed and to locate, evaluate, effectively use, and communicate information in its various formats" (p. 2). The U.S. Department of Labor Secretary's Commission on Achieving Necessary Skills (Whetzel, 1992) identifies information literacy as one of five essential competencies for solid job performance (p. 1). The American Library Association (1996) defines information literacy as simply, "the skills of information problem solving" (p. 1). In its Position Statement on Information Literacy, the ALA quotes the Association for Supervision and Curriculum Development (1996) as saying "information literacy equips individuals to take advantage of the opportunities inherent in the global information society" (p. 1) and urges schools, colleges, and universities to integrate information literacy into all educational programs. "Information Literacy… should be a part of every student's educational experience. ASCD urges schools, colleges, and universities to integrate information literacy programs into learning programs for all students"(p. 1).

While expert definitions of information literacy may vary, one aspect of information literacy teaching is clear: the skills that information literacy provides today's students are critical for future success. Information literacy is not just an assortment of tools that students collect in a tool chest. *It is the tool chest.*

Resource-Based Learning

> "Information literacy, on the other hand, is a potential tool of empowerment for all learners, reached through a 'resource-based' learning approach."
>
> — *Vicki Hancock, 1993, P.1.*

This emphasis on students interacting with and processing information calls for a restructuring of the educational process from passive learning to active learning. Active learning programs require the teacher to adopt a partnership role with students. The teacher assists the student in identifying the desired learner outcomes and then directs the student to the resources that would provide that result. Students become active learners by interacting with information from a variety of resources to produce their own knowledge. In effect, the teacher then becomes a director or coach; students become the star players in their own education. Such programs are often referred to as resource-based learning.

Collaboration and Resource-Based Learning

Resource-based learning requires students to be effective users of information in many formats. To be effective users, students will need *frequent* opportunities to become familiar with print resources, such as books and periodicals, as well as nonprint resources, such as electronic data bases, CDs and the Internet. Teachers and media specialists should work as partners in planning *frequent* experiences in the classroom as well as the school library media center for the students to become skilled at gathering, processing, and reorganizing information to suit their needs. In fact, according to Doiron (1999), many school systems have developed policies "…with resource-based learning as the principal strategy for students using the school library, and cooperative program planning and teaching as the chief method teachers and teacher-librarians use to bring about resource-based learning" (p. 155).

> "Teachers offer direction but do not provide all the information that students need. Instead, they guide students in finding, evaluating, and using information."
> — *Marjorie Warmkessell, 1997, pp. 80-81.*

Information Power's Vision

In its revised edition of *Information Power: Building Partnerships for Learning*, the American Association of School Librarians and the Association for Educational Communications and Technology (1998), described its vision for teachers and media specialists collaborating this way: "…the effective library media specialist draws upon a vision for the student-centered library media program that is based on three central ideas: collaboration, leadership, and technology" (p. 4). This vision of collaboration, leadership, and technology has become central to the mission of the American Association of School Librarians and the Association for Educational Communications and Technology in promoting school librarianship and school library media centers. Around the world, school library media specialists have developed their own mission statements that incorporate these goals and seek to draw patrons into a program of information literacy that is self-directed. The patrons determine the information they wish to research and the media specialist directs them to the resources best suited for their search. As such, media specialists seek collaboration with the classroom teachers who design the curricular content in such a way that students must research the subject matter further to complete their academic goals. In this way, the school library media specialist becomes

> "Without collaboration on the part of the staff, the library is an isolated entity and can't truly function."
> — *Susan Dowling, 1996, p3.*

■ a collaborator with the classroom teacher in planning a project and locating appropriate resources to support it

- an information specialist who directs patrons to the proper resources for searching

- a program administrator who defines the policies of the library media program and directs the activities associated with it and

- a leader in the teaching of information literacy skills.

What are Information Literacy Skills?

In its Position Statement on Information Literacy, the American Library Association (1996) has defined information literacy as "the term being applied to the skills of information problem solving" (p. 1) and goes on to identify seven information problem-solving skills:

Figure 1.3   *The American Library Association's Information Problem-Solving Skills*

1.	Defining the need for information
2.	Initiating the search strategy
3.	Locating the resources
4.	Assessing and comprehending the information
5.	Interpreting the information
6.	Communicating the information
7.	Evaluating the product and process

---

1. Defining the need for information means that an individual recognizes that his or her own knowledge on a subject is inadequate and that resources are available to provide additional data on that subject. The individual then determines what is currently known and what is desired to be known on that subject. And, based on these conclusions, the individual revises a research question.

Figure 1.4   *Defining the Need for Information*

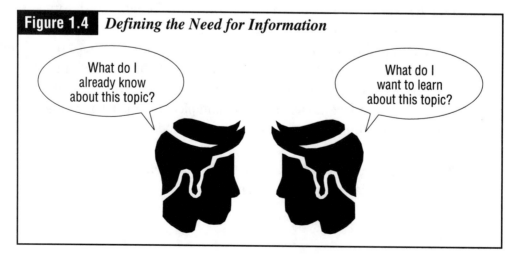

2. Initiating the search strategy is a "presearch" process whereby the individual organizes currently known data into categories or subjects, identifies potential sources of additional material in these categories or subjects and determines criteria for potential sources such as currency, format, and so forth.

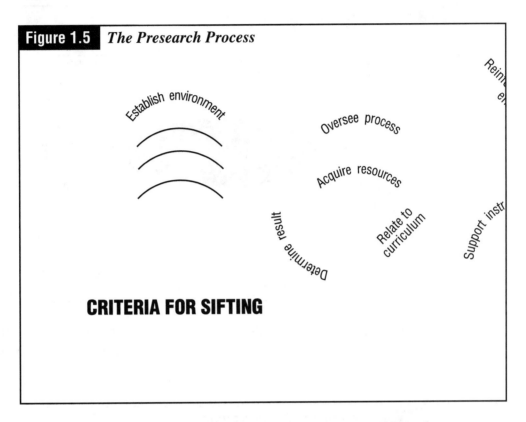

Figure 1.5 *The Presearch Process*

CRITERIA FOR SIFTING

3. Locating the resources is a gathering process wherein the individual searches for print and nonprint resources, online and computerized resources, interviews experts, requests appropriate government documents, and consults with library media specialists and other experts for suggestions of additional resources.

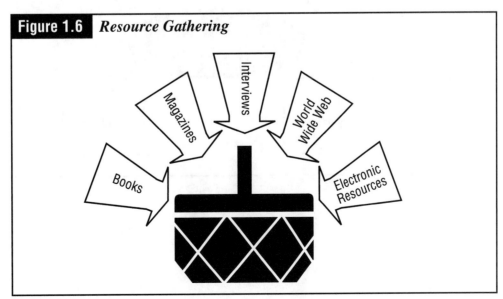

Figure 1.6 *Resource Gathering*

4. Assessing and comprehending the information is an organizing and screening process. The individual skims and scans for keywords and related topics, evaluates authority of resources, identifies errors, opinions, and biases, and then redefines the search question, if necessary.

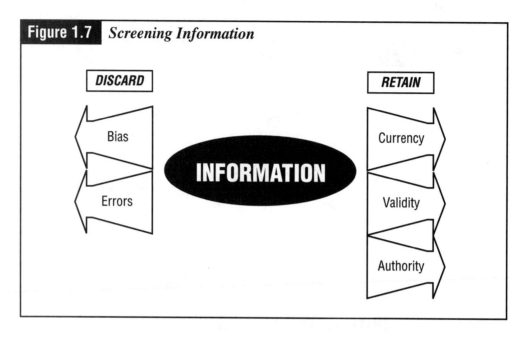

Figure 1.7 *Screening Information*

5. Interpreting the information involves analysis, synthesis, evaluation, and organization of data selected for use and then the derivation of conclusions from the bulk of the research.

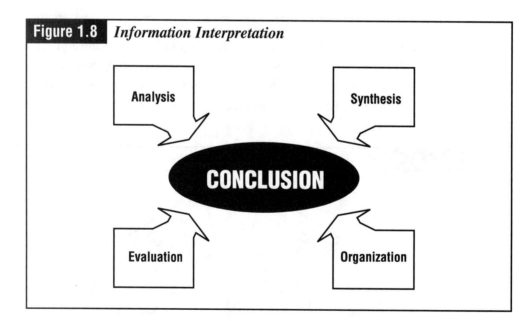

Figure 1.8 *Information Interpretation*

6. *Communication of information* requires an individual to share the information in such a way that others may benefit from the research question. The sharing may be in the form of a report, poster, chart or table, editorial, web page, speech, and so on.

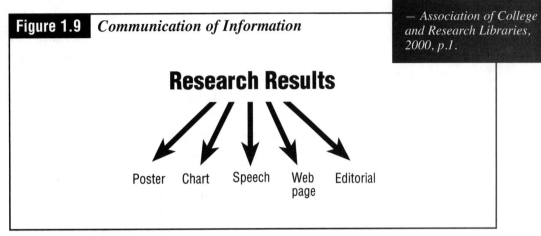

Figure 1.9 *Communication of Information*

Research Results

Poster   Chart   Speech   Web page   Editorial

7. *Evaluation of the product and process* is the final step. The individual determines how well the research data met the defined need and the resulting application of the data.

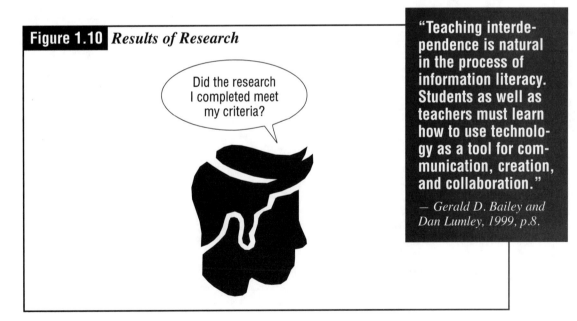

Figure 1.10 *Results of Research*

Did the research I completed meet my criteria?

The ALA concludes that implementing these problem-solving skills requires a restructuring of schools and the learning process. Teachers must change from "textbook lecturers" to "coaches" and learners must become actively involved in their own learning. In its Position Statement on Information Literacy, the ALA identifies this new learning process as resource-based learning (1996, p.1).

The ALA's definition of information literacy and the accompanying skills inherent in becoming information literate are probably the most widely accepted terminology and standards in use today. Since the publication of the American Association of School Librarians and Association for Educational Communications and Technology's *Information Power: Building Partnerships for Learning* in 1998, the AASL and the AECT has taken a stand for library media centers and library media specialists as leaders in the information community in providing access to resources and technology that supply the information needs of students and educators alike.

As media specialists worldwide have adopted the *Information Power* guidelines into their mission statements and programs, one obstacle has arisen in developing information literacy competence in patrons: skill in analyzing the content of library resources requires critical thinking and problem solving abilities. Such skills can be developed only with ***repeated*** opportunities to practice information literacy skills and with continued success in accessing appropriate sources of information. This repetitive practice and high rate of success is critical in determining the effectiveness of any information literacy program or model. This one feature has been missing from some proposed models of teaching information literacy skills and is one that the InfoQuest program inherently addresses.

Chapter *2*

Why Teach Information Literacy?

The pace of information processing in today's society moves at a speed that is continuously accelerating. According to a prediction released by James B. Applebury (1992), Executive Director of the American Association of State Schools and Colleges, the availability of information is growing at such a rate that the current information base is expected to double every 73 days by the year 2020 (p. 8). Information today can not only be generated automatically, but it can also be saved, copied, moved, and otherwise manipulated automatically. Functions that previously took many man-hours are now done automatically. Word processing programs can routinely check for spelling, punctuation, and grammatical errors, and even translate a document into another language and send it to another location. Data that is recorded from a machine into a computer can automatically generate a detailed report. Machines can even be programmed to generate original musical scores, video and graphics.

> "Workers must be equipped not simply with technical know-how but also with the ability to create, analyze, and transform information and to interact effectively with other."
>
> — *Alan Greenspan, 2000, p. 3.*

While this ever-increasing amount of information serves to improve efficiency and productivity in our society, it likewise threatens to overtake us. Nelson (2000) notes that "our proficiency at generating information has exceeded our abilities to find, review, and understand it" (p.1). The sheer volume of data available to us today has transcended the abilities of most people to locate the very data which they need. In other words, the technology to produce data has surpassed the development of tools with which to disseminate it.

The Information Explosion

Terminology for this phenomenon varies, but it has been called Information Overload, Information Explosion, and similar names. The resulting effect on individuals has been dubbed "Information Anxiety" (Wurman, 1989, p. 34). Moreover, as workers strive to keep up with the flow of information on the job, education has lagged behind in preparing individuals to assume roles in this modern workplace where information drives industry.

Figure 2.1 *The Information Explosion*

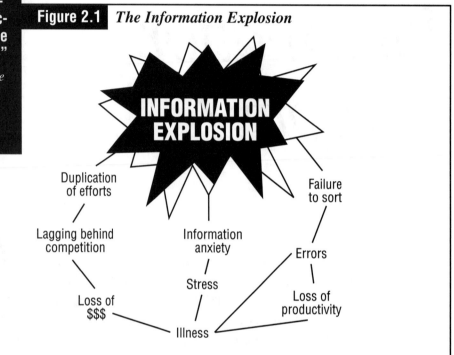

Results of the Information Explosion in the Workplace

The problems caused by this excess of information are legion. When confronted with an abundance of critical data, for example, untrained workers tend to accept the first data available rather than sort through it all. And, this indiscriminate retrieval of information should be no surprise, for the sheer volume of data is overwhelming. John Naisbitt, author of *Megatrends* (1982), says "Scientists who are overwhelmed with technical data complain of information pollution and charge that it takes less time to do an experiment than to find out if it has already been done" (p. 24). The result of this immense volume of data is that individuals are provided with both useful and useless data. Today's workers must be trained to determine the difference.

An additional problem created by sheer volume of data is inaccuracy. With the enormous amount of data available, frequent errors and inconsistencies appear. Without a means to efficiently evaluate the data from similar sources, conflicting data is often reported. Such conflicts coupled with time constraints cause individuals to feel frustrated in trying to determine which part of the data uncovered is valid. Without sorting through data and confirming validity of data, individuals are left with data that is ineffective, erroneous, or worse. Moreover, deriving a conclusion from one's efforts is impossible.

> "They need to know how to be able to gather information from varied sources, synthesize it, interpret it, and evaluate it and unless young people are taught to do this, they will become less than fully participating workers and citizens of the future."
>
> *— Association of College and Research Libraries, 1998, p. 8.*

Results of the Information Explosion in the Schools

Today's students are no less susceptible to this overload of information than are today's workers. They often face similar problems in retrieving data and behave in much the same fashion as today's workers. Lynn Akin (1998) queried students about their responses to being overloaded with information. The students reported headaches, tiredness, depression, frustration, even feeling panicked when overloaded. They also reported that they were likely to skip over data when too much was uncovered. Akin concluded, "It is important for librarians to become aware of information overload and the ways in which students experience it" (p. 8).

Over the past six years, I have observed some alarming trends in student research. Even the brightest students tend to accept the first information they locate on a topic rather than sorting through all available sources to locate the best. Because the first search term they select generally produces some results, students often do no more than a single search. Moreover, teachers in the various schools where I have worked seem to support these "first-results-only" types of searches by limiting the time students are allotted to conduct a search and by encouraging fast results as opposed to a more time-consuming search of all sources, print and nonprint. As a result, student searches frequently begin and end with the Internet, when often a print resource is not only available but more authoritative and even more comprehensive.

> "You must live feverishly in a library. Colleges are not going to do any good unless you are raised and live in a library every day of your life."
>
> *— Ray Douglas Bradbury, 1976, p. 25.*

A recent report by the *New York Times* corroborates this observation. In her article entitled "Choosing Quick Hits over the Card Catalog," Lori Leibovich (2000) reports that today's high school students seem to prefer Internet searches to searching a variety of resources at the library and adds that educators fear that this avoidance of library resources causes students to settle for quick hits with what is often less than desirable results (p. 1).

What's worse, students seem to avoid professional help with their searches. Lubans (1999) reports that even though librarians are the ones best suited to help students be more efficient searchers, "...the bad news is that most students feel they don't need a librarian to help them find resources" (p.1). And even though today's students may do more electronic searching than any other generation, students' search skills don't seem to improve over time. Risko, Alvarez, and Fairbanks (1991) found that "...college juniors and seniors perform much the same as freshmen and sophomores in their general use of library resources" (p. 223).

A recent report released by the Boyer Commission (1999) indicates that today's college graduates are not faring much better. The commission notes that thousands of students graduate from college without developing proper research skills (p. 1).

Perhaps this phenomenon is a reflection of our society's instant gratification trend. Joyce Kasman Valenza (1996) notes that students may "...grossly underestimate the research process, often forgetting the human side of the information picture: the planning, the processing, the thinking, the skills that we label information literacy" (p. 1). And research from Loertscher and Woolls published in an article by Ken Haycock in *Teacher Librarian* (1999) states that..."students typically need more time to 'consume and absorb' the information they find than they are given" (p. 1).

Another alarming trend I have observed is what I call the "re-name it and claim it" process of copying and pasting information. Students seem to feel that because information on the Internet is free and available to all that it is up for grabs. They typically locate a passage they like, and simply copy and paste it into their document. This practice applies to everything from a single phrase to an entire thesis. And, many times, they get away with it simply because it is overly time-consuming for teachers to check every possible source to confirm plagiarism. Haycock (1999) notes, "synthesis, especially summarizing and making decisions rather than copying someone else's ideas and conclusions, must be taught for students in order for them to apply and use this skill set" (p. 1). Sometimes this act of copying another is merely due to a student's lack of confidence in developing his or her own ideas. Hepworth (1999) states that students are more likely to publish their own ideas if they can overcome a "fear of getting it wrong and also a lack of experience in using information to creatively derive their own ideas" (p. 6).

A third trend I have observed is that some students also tend to accept a quantity of sources as acceptable evidence of an adequate search, regardless of the quality of the results. Assuming that quantity indicates thoroughness, students feel that having a large number of sources, whether or not all of them are credible and authoritative, satisfies the need for information. And by failing to identify acceptable standards for the quantity of sources accepted, students fail to consider qualifiers such as currency, authority, validity, bias. A recent study at the University of Michigan (Liebovich, 2000) found that students using big search engines get an overwhelming number of hits and then react by saying something like, "O.K., I found a lot of answers — I'll take the first couple." Liebovich concludes, "That is exactly the kind of attitude that makes some educators worry that students will use the Internet as a quick fix" (p. 3).

These same students, while utilizing technology regularly, are not progressing in developing information literacy competencies. While our students who use technology may not be utilizing it to the fullest, the number of those who do not have access to technology is growing. This gap between the technology "haves" and "have-nots" has been called the Digital Divide.

> "Students set out with a basket and enjoy an information binge, scooping up everything they can find ...confusing quantity and sheer volume of information with success, they greedily scoop up everything within their reach... We must beware of a 'buffet mentality' when we step up to the information feast."
> — *Jamie McKenzie, 1999, p. 2 and 1997, p. 4.*

The Digital Divide

The U.S. Department of Commerce (July, 1999) reports that the Digital Divide currently separates the digitally literate from the digitally illiterate along the lines of education, geography, and income (p.1). And, according to the National Telecommunication Information Administration study, "Falling Through the Net: Defining the Digital Divide," (1999) the gap continues to widen (p. 1). Statistics from this report include:

- 61.6% of college educated adults use the Internet while only 6.6% of adults with a high school diploma or less use the Internet.

- People with a college degree are more than 8 times more likely to own a home computer than those without a college degree.

- 61.8% of married couples own a home computer while only 31.7% of single parents do.

- The digital divide between those at the highest and lowest education levels grew by 25% between 1997 and 1998, and at the same time, the gap for home internet access between whites and blacks grew by 37.7%.

The Digital Divide in Schools

The Digital Divide may be wider than we think. In fact, while there is an acknowledged digital divide between those who have technology and those who do not, there is also a digital divide between teachers who utilize technology in instruction and those who do not. And, the gap is not drawing closer quickly enough. The U.S. Department of Education reported (Carvin, 1999) that only 20% of America's teachers feel comfortable integrating technology into their lesson plans (p. 2). Moreover, of the teachers who have technology available in their classrooms, only 7% had their students use e-mail three or more times per year and fewer still required their students to participate in an online project or publish on the Web (Carvin, 1999, p.3).

If statistics for our K-12 schools appear dismal, our colleges and university statistics are more dismal still. Despite longer hours, more user-friendly atmosphere, greater emphasis on technology and other programs to attract patrons, today's college students may not even use their university libraries. The convenience of owning their own computer with Internet access may be a factor, but certainly not the only one. A 1997 student survey conducted at the Central Queensland University in Sydney, Australia (Orr, Slee, and Evryniadis, 1997, p. 1) revealed that:

■ students do not feel comfortable utilizing electronic facilities to research

■ students do not appreciate visiting academic libraries for their sources

■ many students have no previous experience with academic libraries

Central Queensland University is not unique in this phenomenon. A 1991 study (Risko, Alvarez & Fairbanks) indicated that only 16% of students in a typical university used the library for independent study (p. 222). Donnelley (2000), of York College of Pennsylvania, agrees, saying, "…even though we provided many hours of service, many students never passed through the library's doors" (p. 2). An earlier study (Lyle, 1963) indicated that half of the students who do use the library use it only as a study hall (p. 2). Yet, a typical university library is a major investment for any school. Why are students not taking advantage of this tremendous resource? If Central Queensland University is representative of the status of universities around the world, then, regardless of the recent emphasis on teaching information literacy in our schools, today's students are still at risk for being information illiterate.

In light of these alarming trends among today's students, information literacy instruction is undoubtedly a critical skill that needs greater emphasis in our curricula. Our students must be prepared to graduate from our high schools and colleges and assume a place in the workplace, but without the necessary information processing skills, how prepared will they be?

Technology Literacy

Simply having technology does not mean one is technology literate. Being able to play computer games or use a word processor does not mean one is technology literate. Being able to send e-mail does not mean an individual is technology literate. And many of our nation's teachers cannot even do those things but are expected to incorporate technology into the curriculum. According to the Milken Family Foundation's Progress of Technology in the Schools Report (2000), the average teacher receives less than 13 hours of technology training per year, and 40% of the nation's teachers have received no technology training at all. As a result, our students are not only unable to utilize technology to its fullest, but are often rewarded for utilizing it as little as possible (p. 18).

Benefits of Information Literacy

In light of this and similar observations, the ALA Presidential Committee on Information Literacy asserts that information literacy is considered a skill necessary for survival in today's society for many reasons:

- The quality of life is much higher when an individual is informed about opportunities, alternatives and current events.

- The ability to access information insures that individuals can make wise decisions.

- Information literacy is empowering. Individuals who lack information literacy skills are dependent on others and therefore receive all information second-hand, making it subject to inaccuracy and biased interpretation.

- Informed citizens are able to interact effectively with ideas and values different form their own and thus have a better understanding of the world.

- Informed workers make better employees in a global marketplace.

The need for information which is fueling all aspects of modern society is rapidly changing the way schools are approaching teaching methodology and curriculum standards. No more are stand-up lectures interesting, motivating, or challenging to today's students—instead, these students require participation, investigation, integration with various sources of information. Today's students want and need to be active learners. Active learning does not require students to memorize data and recite facts. Instead, active learning requires students to interact with data; to be informed about theories and ideas; to locate sources of information and be able to analyze and synthesize data.

Learning in the Past vs. Learning Today

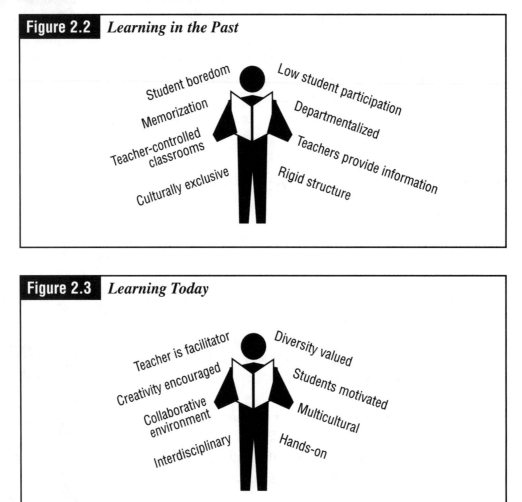

Figure 2.2 *Learning in the Past*

Student boredom
Memorization
Teacher-controlled classrooms
Culturally exclusive
Low student participation
Departmentalized
Teachers provide information
Rigid structure

Figure 2.3 *Learning Today*

Teacher is facilitator
Creativity encouraged
Collaborative environment
Interdisciplinary
Diversity valued
Students motivated
Multicultural
Hands-on

How Students Benefit From Information Literacy Programs

As students become skilled in information literacy, traditional teaching methods are less and less effective media for teachers presenting new concepts and ideas. Rather, students begin to take more control over their own learning, and the teacher begins to move from the image of being an expert in his/her field to being a facilitator of learning experiences. The result is that students:

■ Take an active part in their own learning

■ Find the projects more motivating

■ Show more sustained interest in activities

■ Interact and learn from others with a variety of interests and ability levels

■ Have greater retention of material

■ Develop critical thinking skills in selecting appropriate resources

■ Become skilled in lifelong learning habits

■ Make rapid progress with less fear of failure

Why Teach Information Literacy Using InfoQuest?

A variety of models have been proposed for teaching information literacy skills, but most assume that a student will research for the purpose of producing a product such as a research paper or thesis. While this is a necessary endeavor for upper middle and high school students, it is impractical for younger students in grades K-3. Yet the basis for learning to successfully research must begin earlier so that students can be successful researchers and are less tempted to plagiarize.

InfoQuest is a game of challenging research questions that can be answered in the school library media center. Each week a different question is posed on the intercom and students have all week to come to the media center to research the answer. Younger children are given hints and much more guidance, but all ages are encouraged to participate. Prizes are distributed on Friday for the students who have found the correct answer.

Using a program such as InfoQuest:

- Provides opportunities for active, resource-based learning

- Introduces students to the thrill of being an information detective—it is challenging, motivating, and exciting, even to younger students

- Stimulates interest in a specific subject area or research question

- Helps students distinguish between types of resources

- Assists students in analyzing the suitability of specific resources for providing the desired information—i.e., provides practice in critical thinking skills

- Supports current theories of brain development

- Assists students in documenting their research findings

- Helps students to become successful and independent researchers and thereby be less tempted to plagiarize the research of another

- Empowers students with success

Information Literacy Standards

Chapter 3

In June, 1998, the American Association of School Librarians, a division of the American Library Association, and the Association for Educational Communications and Technology released a second version of *Information Power: Building Partnerships for Learning*. *Information Power* made a strong case for combining leadership, technology, and collaboration among media specialists and classroom teachers. One of the most significant contributions of *Information Power* is the Information Literacy Standards for Student Learning which outlined three categories, nine standards, and 29 indicators that students must master in order to be considered information literate. Those standards are summarized as follows:

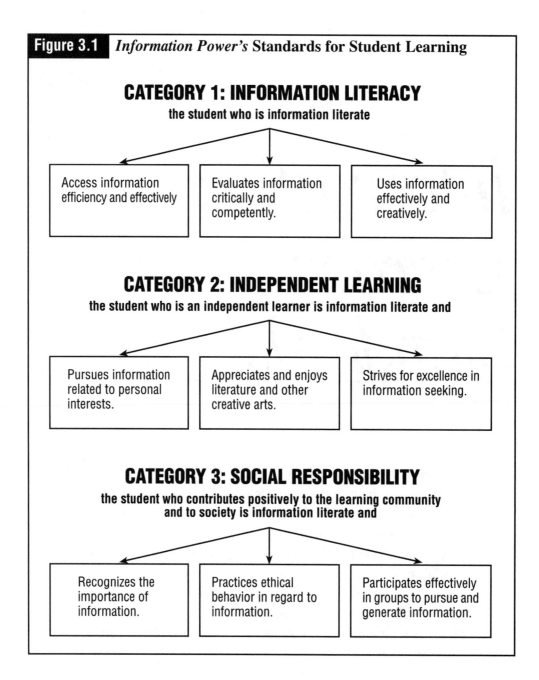

Figure 3.1 *Information Power's* Standards for Student Learning

CATEGORY 1: INFORMATION LITERACY
the student who is information literate

| Access information efficiency and effectively | Evaluates information critically and competently. | Uses information effectively and creatively. |

CATEGORY 2: INDEPENDENT LEARNING
the student who is an independent learner is information literate and

| Pursues information related to personal interests. | Appreciates and enjoys literature and other creative arts. | Strives for excellence in information seeking. |

CATEGORY 3: SOCIAL RESPONSIBILITY
the student who contributes positively to the learning community and to society is information literate and

| Recognizes the importance of information. | Practices ethical behavior in regard to information. | Participates effectively in groups to pursue and generate information. |

School Library Media Centers and the Library Research Service State Studies

The Library and Information Science Program in the College of Education of the University of Denver has partnered with the Colorado State Library and the Colorado Department of Education to staff and support the Library Research Service. Each year a school library media survey is voluntarily completed by public schools in the state of Colorado. Results of this survey were compiled in the latest Colorado study on how school library media centers help student achievement.

Recently, Keith Curry Lance, Christine Hamilton-Pennell, and Marcia J. Rodney with the Library Research Service in Colorado conducted studies in Alaska, Pennsylvania and Colorado on the impact of the school library media programs on student performance. In every case, the results of the studies showed that school library media centers have a significant effect on student performance. In fact, the results indirectly showed support for the principles expounded in *Information Power* and confirmed a positive link between successful school library media programs and student achievement.

The Alaska Study

The Alaska study, released by Keith Curry Lance, et. al. in 1999, was entitled, "Information Empowered: The School Librarian as an Agent of Academic Achievement in Alaska Schools." A summary of results showed that in both elementary and secondary schools in Alaska:

■ Student achievement test scores tend to be higher where there is a school librarian.

■ The length of time the school librarian was available showed a positive correlation to higher student usage and thus higher test scores.

■ The greater number of library staff hours dedicated to delivering library instruction, planning with teachers, and providing in-service to staff, the higher the level of student achievement.

■ The more often that students received library/information literacy instruction by library media staff, the higher the test scores.

■ Test scores were also higher when there was cooperation with a public library, Internet access and a collection policy that addressed reconsideration of materials.

In conclusion, the Alaska study showed that there was a strong, positive relationship between school librarians and test scores that could not be explained away by school size, funding and teacher staffing levels.

The Second Colorado Study

The Alaskan results compared favorably with the results of the study in Colorado, "How School Librarians Help Kids Achieve Standards: the Second Colorado Study," in April 2000. In conducting this study, a follow-up to the 1993 Colorado study entitled "The Impact of School Library Media Centers on Academic Achievement," Keith Curry Lance and his team found that:

■ student reading achievement test scores increased with increases in program development, information technology, teacher and library media specialist collaboration, and individual student visits to the media center.

■ As media specialists took on leadership roles, collaboration increased.

■ Students perform at higher levels when their access to the Media Center is not tied in to regularly scheduled classes, but as they have a need to come.

Again, these results corroborate the vision of *Information Power* in supporting collaboration, leadership, and technology for school library media specialists and showed that when school library media specialists collaborate with classroom teachers and when the media program is well-funded, well-staffed and flexibly scheduled, student achievement rises. Moreover, these results were not explained away by differences in school communities, district expenditures, teacher/pupil ratios, teacher experience, or demographics.

The Pennsylvania Study

The third study, entitled "Measuring Up to Standards: The Impact of School Library Media Programs and Information Literacy in Pennsylvania Schools," released by Keith Lance, et. al, (2000) corroborated the findings of the two other studies and also found that the size of the collection has proved to be an indicator of student achievement as well as frequency of use, amount of expenditures, number of technological resources, and how technology is integrated into programs. When all library predictors are maximized, student reading scores tend to run 10 to 15 points higher.

The results of these studies have proved the importance of well-staffed, high-service school library media center programs, and they have indirectly supported the vision of collaboration, leadership, and technology as well as the information literacy standards for student learning proposed by the AASL and AECT in *Information Power*. As further studies are conducted, even more support for information literacy standards can be expected.

Nationwide, a variety of school systems have developed a K-12 information literacy curricula, and even colleges and universities have developed courses for information literacy programs. A wide variety of information literacy models have been developed, but media specialists often find the implementation of some of them a bit challenging. Exactly how does one teach first graders the difference between a search engine and a directory? What information literacy skills are appropriate for high-schoolers? What resources are appropriate for teacher/media specialist collaboration on a science project? How does a media specialist teach students who speak English as a second language to do Boolean searches? And most importantly, with all the emphasis on information literacy, why do we continue to graduate students who not only use the internet almost exclusively for research, but also accept the first five hits from an internet search engine as sufficient research?

> "The central job of schools is to maximize the capacity of each student."
>
> — *Carol Ann Tomlinson, 2000, p. 7.*

The answers to these and many other questions related to the development of information literacy skills depend upon the program that is implemented to teach information literacy. Many teaching models have been proposed, but some of the models describe a process for achieving information literacy without identifying *specific* skills at each level for making progress toward that end. Moreover, the emphasis of some of these models is on the product of the process, more than the process itself. Whenever the product is stressed above the process, students typically seek the most direct route to the end result, whatever the cost; the result is that reusing previous efforts, plagiarizing, copying papers from others and more are implemented to simply produce a product that meets with the teacher's approval. And, when the product is a research paper once a year from approximately grades 7-12, how effective can the results be?

Keys to Success Using the InfoQuest Model

The InfoQuest model is based on a philosophy of how to develop information literacy skills without focusing mainly on the product that results. In other words, it is a ***process-oriented*** program. Students are freed from the constraints behind having to perform and thus can focus their efforts on developing skills. Instructors are freed from having to evaluate the products of students' efforts and thus are free to simply direct and evaluate student progress. The result is that students enjoy the process and are ***motivated*** to continue with the program, developing the necessary skills to become information literate.

> "Students learn best when they can make a connection between the curriculum and their interests and life experiences."
>
> — *Carol Ann Tomlinson, 2000, p. 7.*

> **"Effective library and information skills instructional programs not only help students acquire the skills they will need to solve their information problems, but also stimulate intellectual curiosity and encourage continued information seeking and exploration."**
>
> *— Ruth V. Small, 1998, p. 1.*

Modern educators are quick to admit that motivation has a profound effect on learning and performance, but how motivated can a student be to produce yet another research paper year after year? My experience with even the most reluctant students indicates that most are naturally curious and eager to gain knowledge on subjects that interest them. Why not harness that natural curiosity to encourage a skill that is necessary in today's society? When students desire knowledge for the sake of knowing and no more, there is no pressure to perform and avoid failure. Students are free to develop skills at their own pace and as they are able. This is truly *individualized learning*.

Traditionally, students who know exactly what is expected of them perform better. Yet few teachers communicate to students what makes an ideal research project. Why is one thesis more well-supported than another? What qualities of writing indicate a higher level of performance? What determines an "A?" These subjective criteria are exactly what makes research frustrating to students and often kills their desire to learn research skills.

On the other hand, if the expectancy is that students will pursue gathering information on topics that interest them, there is a much higher level of success for all. Who can fail to find learning more about a *personal interest* rewarding? Moreover, the skill of information gathering around one's interests has a practical application for real-life. Outside of school, information gathering is done either on the job, which is generally related to one's personal interests and skills, or for personal enrichment. Why not develop *skills for life*, rather than skills that will be little used outside of the school environment?

> **"Students work best when researching a subject or issue they care about—one that has consequences in their world."**
>
> *— Gerald D. Bailey and Dan Lumley, 1999, p. 2.*

Emotions have a strong effect on learning. What could be more crippling than the fear of failure, and what could be more motivating than a situation where one is not set up to fail? Studies have shown that complex learning is impaired by threat but encouraged by challenges. InfoQuest is continuously challenging and motivating. Students do not fear failure, as they are not critiqued in the same way as they would be in completing a research paper or project. With the crippling effect of fear of failure overcome, students of all ages are free to progress and develop complex search skills as early as they begin the program. For older students, the progress is rapid due to the *ongoing practice* involved.

Information literacy skills must be taught on a continuous basis beginning as early as formal education begins. Students need early and repeated interactions with media specialists who can direct their research until they become competent independent searchers. Student progress toward that goal must be continuously measured and evaluated. A once-a-year research paper beginning in middle or high school is not sufficient experience for today's students. *Guided research that is both challenging and motivating is needed instead.*

S.T.A.I.R.S.

InfoQuest is designed to work with children's natural curiosity and to motivate them to learn more. It is as motivating to young children as it is to teens and adults. The InfoQuest model proposes that there are steps to becoming skilled researchers, but that information can be found at all skill levels. Some means of obtaining information will be more sophisticated as students progress, but the emphasis is on the process more than the product. These steps may be appropriately named S.T.A.I.R.S.—"Steps To Achieving Independent Research Skills." In this research model, students progress along four basic steps:

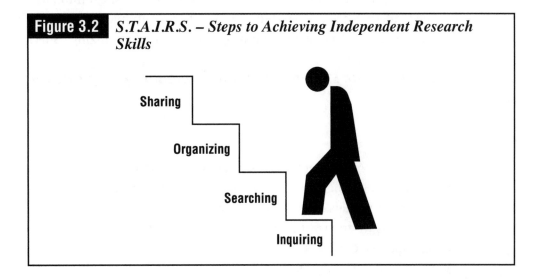

Figure 3.2 | *S.T.A.I.R.S. – Steps to Achieving Independent Research Skills*

Inquiring: In this step, students determine the keywords and related topics in a research question.

Searching: This is the actual search process, where students select and utilize specific resources to gather information.

Organizing: Students logically organize the results of their search, discarding unrelated results and retaining only pertinent information.

Sharing: Students communicate the results, with communication as simple as "I found the answer! It is… " to sharing an entire thesis. Again, the emphasis is on the process more than the product, the knowing as opposed to the lack of knowledge.

Using S.T.A.I.R.S., specific skills along a continuum of information literacy are laid out in the tables below.

Skills Continuum

The following skills continuum is a compilation of skills from a variety of sources, including some of those published as standards for a number of states, suggestions from colleagues, as well as those gleamed from my own 25 years of teaching experience. Assuming that there is some overlap within levels and assuming that all skills will not be achieved at the lower end of a level, but should be attained by the end of a level, teachers and media specialists can use the following continuum of literacy skills as a means of planning for and assessing student progress toward information literacy. And, an InfoQuest program can be implemented to achieve these objectives.

The skills are mapped out in the following levels: Preliminary, Beginner, Intermediate, Advanced. The levels are subdivided into clusters of skills related to the four steps: Inquiring, Searching, Organizing, Sharing.

Step I—Inquiring: The student desires information on a particular subject.

The Preliminary student

- realizes that
    - ❑ the library media center is a source of information
    - ❑ the library media specialist is a source of information
    - ❑ other individuals are a source of information
- shows pleasure in visiting the library media center
    - ❑ in supervised groups
    - ❑ in unsupervised groups
    - ❑ individually
- demonstrates responsibility in use of library media center materials
- knows how to correctly
    - ❑ handle books
    - ❑ handle magazines
    - ❑ handle newspapers
- knows correct procedure for
    - ❑ borrowing a book
    - ❑ returning a book
- can identify
    - ❑ favorite author
    - ❑ favorite illustrator
    - ❑ favorite book character(s)
    - ❑ favorite story
    - ❑ favorite series
- can summarize favorite story
- can describe favorite character
- can communicate what he/she wants to know

- recognizes that the catalog provides information about
  - title
  - author

The Beginner student has achieved all of the above and:

- realizes that
  - books are a source of information
  - magazines are a source of information
  - newspapers are a source of information
  - computer databases are a source of information
  - the World Wide Web is a source of information
  - sources can be both print and nonprint
- is acquainted with the media center staff
- feels comfortable seeking help from the media center staff
- feels comfortable helping others
- knows how to correctly
  - handle computer equipment
  - handle audiovisual equipment
- can identify favorite fiction and nonfiction titles
- can identify fiction authors
- can identify nonfiction authors
- can accurately formulate a question
- can restate a question in own words
- can formulate a list of related topics
- recognizes that a catalog provides information about
  - a subject
  - related subjects
  - a summary of content

The Intermediate student has achieved all of the above and:

- realizes that
  - print and nonprint sources serve different functions
  - the same source can vary in print and nonprint formats
  - sources of information can be primary or secondary
  - the best sources of information fit specific criteria
- visits the library media center frequently for both pleasure and research purposes
- visits the library media center for sources other than electronic media
- feels comfortable in the library media center either working independently or with a group
- knows correct procedure for
  - placing a book on reserve
  - placing a hold on a book
- can identify call numbers for fiction
- can identify call numbers for non-fiction
- can identify a classic American literature title

- can identify a classic American literature author
- can refine a question (broaden or narrow)
- can relate what is known to what is desired to be known
- can brainstorm a list of possible sources of information
- recognizes that a catalog provides information about
  - illustrator
  - publisher
  - copyright date

The Advanced student has achieved all of the above and:

- realizes that
  - criteria can help in selection of appropriate sources
  - related sources can provide additional sources of information
  - sources that provide related but inappropriate information should be discarded
- uses time purposefully in library media center without supervision
- demonstrates pleasure
  - reading
  - browsing
  - utilizing electronic resources and other media
- knows correct procedure for
  - searching other library catalogs and databases
  - ordering materials through an interlibrary loan
- can identify
  - location of classic world literature in media center
  - a list of classic world literature titles
  - classic world literature authors
  - publication periods for classic world literature
  - classic world literature genres (poetry, plays, literature, essays)
- can formulate
  - a research question
  - related themes or ideas
  - a theory to test
  - philosophy based on personal beliefs to support with research
- recognizes that the catalog provides
  - information to help locate a source
  - bibliographical information
  - related resources on a topic

Step II—Searching: The student applies specific strategies for locating information on a subject.

The Preliminary student:

- realizes that
  - the library media center houses a variety of materials
  - materials in library media center are organized for easy access

- can identify location of
  - ☐ fiction books
  - ☐ nonfiction books
- correctly identifies
  - ☐ title of a book
  - ☐ author of a book
  - ☐ subject of a book
- demonstrates knowledge of Dewey Decimal system
- can put books in order by
  - ☐ first number
  - ☐ first and second number
  - ☐ three or more numbers
- can alphabetize by
  - ☐ one letter
  - ☐ two letters
  - ☐ three or more letters
- locates word in a simple dictionary
- locates word and meaning in a simple dictionary
- can demonstrate use of a book to locate information
- recognizes different types of books
- knows location of different types of books in library media center
- uses a dictionary to locate a word
- can identify the name of a source
- can locate a subject in an encyclopedia
- can use a mouse to
  - ☐ point and click
  - ☐ open and close
  - ☐ manipulate desktop icons

The Beginner student has achieved all of the above and

- can locate different types of resources with guidance
- can brainstorm for ideas related to a subject
- can arrange books in order by
  - ☐ one decimal
  - ☐ two decimals
  - ☐ three or more decimals
- can identify subject headings
- can identify subheadings
- can skim or scan for information
- reads captions for information
- can use table of contents
- can use index
- can give main idea of story
- can identify subject of a magazine article
- uses a thesaurus to locate a synonym or antonym
- uses an almanac to locate a statistic

- uses an atlas to find map information
- uses a compass rose for orientation on a map
- can interpret a map key
- can interpret information from
  - a chart
  - a graph
  - a table
  - a picture
- in a dictionary
  - locates word origin
  - locates part of speech
  - uses guide words
  - uses entry words
  - uses root words
  - uses context clues to select the appropriate meaning
- demonstrates careful use of instructional media (projectors, video or audiocassette players)
- after viewing a videotape
  - can state purpose for viewing
  - can identify main idea
- selects appropriate reading material
- can use the computer to
  - locate files
  - open files
  - save files
  - delete files
  - move files
  - rename files
  - print documents
- can utilize
  - word processing programs
  - presentation programs
- can log on to the Internet and
  - use a browser
  - send and receive e-mail
  - use proper netiquette
  - use a search engine
- can use a mouse to
  - drag and drop
  - highlight
  - open, close, or otherwise manipulate desktop icons
  - cut, paste, copy, and perform other editing functions
- can perform an electronic search
  - using keywords

The Intermediate student has achieved all of the above and

- can identify the location of
  - reference books
  - periodicals
  - computer software
  - audiovisual resources
  - catalog to locate resources
- can relate original idea to similar ideas for searching
- uses titles to determine if subject matter is suitable
- uses subtitles, subheadings to determine if subject matter is suitable
- compares information from various sources
- in a dictionary
  - uses pronunciation key
  - uses syllabication and accent marks
  - uses tenses
  - uses parts of speech
  - uses word origins
- uses keywords as a search strategy
- uses see and see also references in an index or catalog
- performs electronic searches using different browsers
- uses Boolean search strategy
- determines distance using a map scale
- demonstrates use of different types of maps (political, physical, contour, etc.)
- after viewing a videotape, can identify supporting details
- after listening to an audiotape, can identify supporting details
- selects materials of appropriate length to complete a project
- can use a computer to
  - organize files into folders
  - back up files
  - create a shortcut to files
  - find files
  - resize windows
  - get help
  - use keyboard shortcuts
- can utilize
  - database programs
  - spreadsheet programs
  - multimedia programs
- can perform an electronic search
  - using Boolean search strategies
  - using quotation marks and parentheses
- can demonstrate careful use of peripherals (printers, scanners, cameras)
- can convert files into multimedia format

The Advanced student has achieved all of the above and

- can locate resources using either the Dewey or LC cataloging format
- can narrow or broaden a topic
- can determine specific criteria to fit topic researched
- uses a variety of reference tools including gazetteers, chronologies, indices, and more
- uses collective and individual biographies for reference purposes
- uses a variety of reference tools on a single research endeavor and knows the purpose of each
- uses media such as video and audio players and tapes to gain information
- uses proofreading tools in a word processor to correct errors
- selects appropriate content related to search criteria
- compares and contrasts information from various sources to determine contradictions
- compares and contrasts information from various sources to determine validity
- compares and contrasts information from various sources to determine bias
- determines when an appropriate amount of research material has been gathered to support a topic
- performs an electronic search
  - ☐ using a variety of search engines and directories
  - ☐ using truncation
  - ☐ using phraseology
  - ☐ using a combination of advanced skills and strategies
- demonstrates respect for legal and ethical use of technology

Step III—Organizing: The student organizes the results of a search for information.

The Preliminary student

- can tell a teacher or media specialist what he/she has learned
- can state findings in own words
- can put events in proper order
- can use a storyboard to sequence a story
- can select a format for presenting ideas
  - ☐ can draw a picture
  - ☐ can make a simple chart
  - ☐ can draw a short timeline of events
  - ☐ can summarize important details
- can compose a title for a story, picture, or chart
- distinguishes between "real" and "pretend"
- can sequence information learned through listening or watching for a purpose

The Beginner student has achieved all of the above and:

- sequences a series of historical events in proper order
- compares and contrasts
- selects topic sentence
- writes own topic sentence
- utilizes graphic organizers for search results
- utilizes outline for search results
- utilizes draw and paint programs to illustrate information learned
- utilizes word processing programs to organize information
- after listening to an audiotape,
  - □ states purpose for listening
  - □ identifies main idea
- paraphrases information located in a resource
- proofreads for
  - □ spelling errors
  - □ for punctuation errors
  - □ for grammatical errors

The Intermediate student has achieved all of the above and:

- recognizes bias
- identifies irrelevant statements
- skims/scans for information
- recognizes criteria for evaluation: currency, authority, validity, and so forth.
- judges suitability of a resource for project
- utilizes note cards to organize search results
- correctly compiles bibliographical information
- correctly compiles citations
- quotes correctly
- paraphrases correctly
- summarizes and credits author correctly
- utilizes word processing tools to organize information gathered
  - □ formats with columns
  - □ formats with tabs
  - □ indents paragraphs
  - □ creates headers and footers
  - □ creates master page for document
- organizes thoughts in a web
- utilizes spreadsheets to organize facts and data gathered
  - □ utilizes spreadsheet functions to create a chart or graph
  - □ formats a key for chart or graph
  - □ labels axis for chart or graph
- summarizes information found in a chart, graph or table
- distinguishes between fact and opinion
- correctly identifies different types of writing: narrative, persuasive, and so forth

- utilizes databases to organize facts and data gathered
- utilizes databases to organize bibliographical information
- correctly prepares a timeline, graph, chart, or table
- writes notes on main ideas located in a resource
- uses notes to organize information into an outline of reference material
- can outline and use notes to write paragraph in own words
- proofreads for omissions, insertions, indentations, tense, and other errors

The Advanced student has achieved all of the above and

- can organize results of previous electronic searches using bookmarks and folders
- determines when an appropriate number of resources have been gathered to support a project
- selects most appropriate format for relaying information gathered
- utilizes a variety of tools and software programs to organize information

Step IV: Sharing. *The student effectively shares knowledge learned through his/her research efforts. The emphasis is more on the learning process rather than a specific product.*

The Preliminary student:

- demonstrates reaction to story by creating a picture
- can give a short speech in front of the class
- clearly presents information learned
- presents information learned in sequence
- utilizes charts, graphs, and pictures to illustrate points
- notes location of information learned
- shows others how to locate same information
- retells information in order in his/her own words

The Beginner student has achieved all of the above and:

- determines how to best share information learned
- orally retells key points learned
- participates in a group discussion on material learned
- prepares a newscast, speech, or narrates a documentary audiotape
- integrates multimedia and Internet sources into a presentation
- writes information learned in own words in editorial, newsletter, report, etc.
- visually displays information learned in a poster, videotape, slide show, chart, graph, table
- sequences events appropriately
- retells events in own words
- communicates information in complete sentences
- writes appropriate topic sentences
- organizes sentences into paragraphs
- writes appropriate headings
- organizes paragraphs in order

- creates appropriate title for work
- edits
- proofreads

The Intermediate student has achieved all of the above and

- determines appropriate format for presentation
- determines appropriate mode of oral or written presentation
  - ☐ descriptive
  - ☐ narrative
  - ☐ persuasive
- if appropriate, effectively uses literary devices in presentation
  - ☐ dialogue
  - ☐ figurative language
  - ☐ foreshadowing
- supports all points made with effective, authoritative statistics
- creates original visual aids to display information
- composes introduction
- composes conclusion
- correctly formats bibliography
- correctly writes footnotes, citations, and references in MLA or APA style, if necessary
- creates and maintains a web page to share information

The Advanced student has achieved all of the above and

- self-monitors presentation to stay within time limits
- designs presentation to reflect specific criteria
- fits presentation to audience
- integrates appropriate media into presentation
  - ☐ uses multimedia authoring tools
  - ☐ utilizes Internet resources
  - ☐ utilizes visual aids
- appropriately cites resources used

Following a research model without a list of skills to attain is akin to taking a journey to an unknown destination without a road map.

Chapter 4

How To Teach Information Literacy More Effectively

Educators and experts alike have agreed that information skills are necessary for students to be successful in today's society. Many models have been proposed on how to go about teaching information literacy skills in the curriculum. The previous chapter outlined the InfoQuest model and defined specific information literacy skills in graduated levels in accordance with four steps or stages in researching.

In 1995, the ALA Presidential Committee on Information Literacy (April 17, 1995) called for individual State Departments of Education, Commissions on Higher Education and Academic Governing Boards to ensure that information literacy is a part of each state curriculum (p. 18). In accordance with this stance, many states such as Wisconsin, Minnesota, Washington, and others have developed a statewide curriculum initiative for information literacy skills and continue to promote their importance throughout the curriculum. Statistics such as those from the Library Research Service studies on the impact of library media programs in the states of Alaska, Pennsylvania, and Colorado (1999, 2000) repeatedly demonstrate the significance of media service programs and their correlation to higher student achievement (p.93–94). Groups such as the American Library Association, the American Association of School Librarians, the Association for Educational Communications and Technology and the Association for Supervision and Curriculum Development continue to stress the importance of information literacy skills in the total curriculum.

Nevertheless, teachers in all grade levels and in nearly every subject area repeatedly assign research projects, and, year after year, students dutiful-

> **"Close collaboration between teacher and teacher librarian of an equal status provide the best approach to effective library use and resource-based learning."**
>
> *— Michael Marland, 1999, p. 54.*

ly churn them out. But students continue to graduate from our best schools with insufficient training in information literacy skills. David V. Loertscher and Blanche Woolls (1997) reported that "to date, the research shows we are not making great strides teaching students or teachers to handle new oceans of information currently available to most students" (p.23). Earlier, Judy Pitts (1995) noted that "...students were not overwhelmed by too much information. Instead, they were floating in a sea of information but did not know how to access more than a few drops" (p.181).

Not only are our students showing less progress in developing information literacy skills than we have hoped, they seem to be avoiding the very resources that could help them do so. Statistics released by the ALA in its Presidential Committee on Information Literacy report (1995) indicate that 25% of all undergraduates spend no time in the library during a normal week, and that 65% use the library four hours or less per week (p.6). Why?

Some schools lack sufficient funding for technology and library media center resources. In an article entitled, "How Do You Measure Up?" by Dr. Marilyn Miller and Dr. Marilyn Shontz, *School Library Journal* (1999) reported that the range of school expenditures on media programs vary widely, with one of our nation's schools reporting annual spending of only $330 (p. 3). In addition, Miller and Shontz report that spending for AV materials on the average has declined while spending on media and software has been "weak" (p. 7).

> **"Technology must become part of the curriculum. Students must develop an understanding of how technology influences our lives."**
>
> *— Gerald D. Bailey and Dan Lumley, 1999, p. 8.*

Schools in some systems have been forced to cut back on library media center programs. In too many districts, library media specialists are understaffed and overworked. Program cuts in some areas have forced media specialists to work unassisted or to work at more than one school, dividing their time equally between two programs. According to Miller and Shontz (1999), most schools continue to be staffed by only one library media specialist and at least 10% of school library media specialists only work part-time (p. 1). Data reported by the National Council on Educational Statistics (Rowand, 1999) indicates that 23.9 % of schools responding to the 1999 survey had library media specialists with no degree. Worse, the same survey indicated that 446 schools participating in the survey reported no library at all (p. 33).

The reasons for less than adequate information literacy programs vary from state to state, from school district to school district, from school to school and even from teacher to teacher, but one common variable in the application of information literacy skills remains: classroom teachers often feel inadequate to initiate information literacy strategies with their students because many feel inadequate in locating information themselves. Many shy away from searching because they are hesitant about using an autocat, electronic resources, the Internet, or other technology tools to assist in a search.

And this discomfort with technology carries over into their lessons. According to the US Department of Education in a report released in February 1999, only 20% of America's teachers feel comfortable in integrating technology into their lessons (Andy Carvin, 1999, p.3).

Library Media Specialists Can Help Schools Utilize Technology More Fully

Library media specialists, on the other hand, are the individuals in each school whose special training in utilizing technology and information-seeking strategies should make them a valuable resource in assisting classroom teachers. Troy Swanson (2000), in an editorial for *American Libraries* calls librarians "…knowledge managers, information specialists, chief answerists, knowledge navigators" (p. 32). But in spite of their specialized training and desire to help, library media specialists frequently meet strong resistance in collaborative planning for information literacy activities. "We're the ones that provide content and meaning to the rhythms created by the technologists," says Swanson (p. 32). But Swanson acknowledges that librarians' expertise is not always valued. "The problem is, it's cool to be linked to technology but not cool to be librarians," he muses (p. 32). And this is very often the case in our schools. In places where the contribution of the school library media specialist is not perceived as essential, some teachers see the library media specialist as no more than a "special" teacher that relieves them for a planning period.

> "The teacher-librarian's role is to facilitate and maximize student and staff access to a broad range of resources."
> — *Mary Tarasoff and Sonya Emperingham, 1999, p. 215.*

Fixed scheduling of library media center time supports this attitude on behalf of teachers, as research skills are taught in isolation; as such, fixed scheduling has not proved to be conducive to the development of information literacy skills. Teachers in such schools rarely see collaboration with the media specialist as a necessary initiative. In fact, even where flexible scheduling is the norm, collaboration may not occur. According to Miller and Shontz (1999), the amount of time spent in collaborative planning between classroom teachers and library media specialists has been in a "disturbing decline" (p. 13). More innovative classroom teachers may want to join in collaborative activities but feel pressured to fulfill curricular standards and have little time or interest in developing new programs. Regardless, collaborative planning between library media specialists and classroom teachers, particularly the 80% of the nations' instructors who feel uncomfortable utilizing technology, should help overcome the in-school digital divide.

Collaboration is the Key

Savvy library media specialists can begin to initiate programs with classroom teachers by picking up where classroom teachers leave off. Through attending grade-level meetings and curricular planning sessions, library media specialists can learn the units of study for specific grade levels and classes and plan accordingly. They can gear activities to supplement the materials used in the classroom. Library media specialists can suggest related materials and ideas. They can anticipate upcoming events (such as annual science fairs or programs, field trips, debates, etc.) and offer services. They can involve teachers in the selection of new materials. And, by building a relationship with the classroom teachers, library media specialists can promote the necessity of providing information-seeking strategies in order to prepare students for the future. Collaboration can occur even when a classroom teacher does not take the initiative to seek help from the media specialist.

Teacher/Library Media Specialist Collaboration Model

The following model depicts the role of the classroom teacher and the school library media specialist in collaboration on information literacy projects. The classroom teacher should:

■ establish the environment and parameters of a research project (to be done in class, outside of class, using LMC resources, using Internet resources, using primary resources, etc.)

■ determine the audience and arrangement of the project (i.e., individual students, pairs, teams, etc.)

■ relate the project to the curriculum (particularly if it is across content areas)

■ determine the expected results (method of sharing, length, tone, point of view, content, etc.)

The library media specialist should assume an equal but supportive role in completing a research project as follows:

■ support and enrich classroom instruction

■ acquire the appropriate resources (locate appropriate websites, purchase materials, utilize interlibrary loans, etc.)

- oversee the process by reserving computers, software and other resource materials, setting times for class visits and bibliographic instruction, determine appropriateness of resources

- reinforcing student research efforts (encouraging successful students and helping to direct unsuccessful students down a different path)

"First, teacher-librarians must be prepared to initiate planning with teachers, rather than waiting for teachers to come to them."

— *Carol-Ann Page, 1999, p. 189.*

Both classroom teachers and library media specialists should:

- model information literacy skills

- guide student practice and

- ensure appropriate teaching.

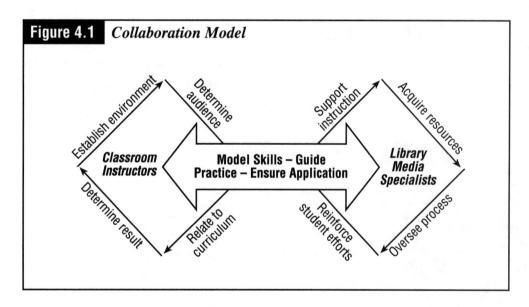

Figure 4.1 *Collaboration Model*

Often the drive to become information literate begins with a desire on the part of the students themselves to utilize technology and innovative resources — a sort of "if you provide it, they will come" philosophy. If library media centers can offer adequate technology and exciting media to utilize in researching, students will be eager to take advantage of it. Most students are naturally curious. Few are as inhibited as adults in trying out something new. When encouraged, students are interested in returning to activities in which they have experienced success. Students' curiosity coupled with success in searching makes seeking information intrinsically motivating, which is the key to successfully operating a program that will carry over into student's lives outside of school.

Motivation—the Missing Factor

> "Turn assignments into more engaging problems. The higher the students' interest is at the outset, the more likely they are to spend more time on the task."
>
> — *David Loertscher, 1999, p. 150.*

This intrinsic motivation is the missing factor in many information literacy programs and models. *How many students are truly motivated to complete yet another research report?* However, if students are interested in accessing materials and discovering ideas, they will find a way to do so. If the students are successful in their quest, they will find it pleasurable and will want to do so again and again. Ruth Small (1998) notes that "library media specialists can employ strategies that stimulate curiosity about a topic of interest at the beginning of and throughout the research process" (p. 6). Once curiosity has been piqued, then sufficient repetition to develop adequate skills is the key to building habits of a lifetime — lifelong learning. Motivation, repetition and reinforcement are the key reasons why the InfoQuest program is successful. It is based on the PROBE method of research.

The PROBE Method

To help students develop into lifelong learners, who are informed citizens and successful employees, educators must design a learning environment that motivates students to PROBE for information— that is:

Figure 4.2	*The Probe Method*

*P*rovide an information-rich environment
*R*equire activities where students must seek information
*O*ffer multiple opportunities to practice information-seeking
*B*ring attention to a variety of information sources
*E*ncourage the information seekers

> "Ideally, effective library and information skills instruction not only helps students acquire the skills they need to be able to solve their information problems, but also stimulates and encourages intellectual curiosity, information-seeking, and exploration behaviors."
>
> — *Ruth Small, 1999, p. 1.*

Provide an information-rich environment.

Information literacy skills cannot be taught without the necessary tools with which to locate information. Schools need to provide a well-stocked media center as well as a variety of tools, and teach students the advantages and disadvantages of each. Computer databases are an excellent source of information and are very popular with students, as information can be located rapidly. However, many databases do not provide full-text documents or accompanying photos, while others, because they are subject-specific or audience-specific cannot meet every need. CDs are another popular source of information and are relatively inexpensive and easy to use. However, once again, research CDs are subject-specific and therefore of limited use. Information specialists must purchase reference CDs that relate not only to the curriculum, but also curriculum changes. Many CDs become scratched or otherwise damaged and are no longer useful. And not all CDs are networkable — and are therefore limited to a single user at a time. Print resources are not as popular as they used to be before the advent of computers networks and e-books, but books provide a wealth of information, are easily searchable and often contain more illustrations, charts, graphs, and so on than online resources. Often print resources contain a bibliography, which can lead to additional sources of information related to a research topic. And print resources can sometimes put more information in the hands of more students at one time than online resources which are limited to the number of computer workstations available, the number of printers available, and whether or not the resources are networked or limited to a single user.

> "The school which practices inquiry-centered approaches to learning requires much more personnel, resources and space for the same number of students than a school which stresses textbook-oriented Socratic methods."
>
> — *Ken Haycock, 1999, p. 63.*

Schools need to be prepared to provide a reasonable number of computer workstations and the network resources for them. (The most desirable number of workstations should be based on total enrollment as well as the conditions under which these workstations will be used.) The media center and its resources should be current, attractive, suited to the audience and the curriculum, and available during the hours in which students may need access to them.

As government and private sources are becoming aware of the "digital divide" — the imaginary line which separates those who have access to technology and those who do not, programs and money are being poured into closing the gap. Programs such as the Federal Communications Commission's Universal Service Fund, The Clinton-Gore e-Rate, and The Bill and Melinda Gates Foundation have channeled dollars into technology and telecommunications services for both public and private schools across the country. Programs such as the national e-rate have provided funding for schools to acquire telephone and internet connectivity. Bill and Melinda Gates have developed their own foundation to donate funds for school technology. For schools, the opportunity to acquire technology and related resources has never been greater. Media specialists might seek out sources of funding, apply for technology grants, partner with a large corporate donor, or otherwise seek to take advantage of such opportunities. The last part of this chapter discusses more fully a number of such opportunities for fund raising.

Require students to seek interesting information

Students are naturally curious, but their curiosity is often squelched by the good intentions of educators who require students to research dull topics in which the students have little interest. If students are curious, they are eager to research. Requiring students to do regular research is easy when it is

> "With hundreds of computers and dozens of classrooms connected to extensive electronic information resources, schools are recognizing the importance of reinventing the way they engage students in both questioning and research."
>
> *— Jamie McKenzie, 1999, p. 1.*

a matter of piquing their curiosity. This is what InfoQuest is all about — piquing students' curiosity. Each week an intriguing question is posed school-wide on the intercom. Students are motivated by the interest shown among their peers and by their teachers. Researching the answer to the question becomes a game. Requiring participation is more about encouraging than forcing and students become eager participants. Even the most reluctant students are easier to motivate when given a little encouragement to participate by being reminded of the rewards or seeing others successfully finding the answer.

Offer multiple opportunities to practice information seeking strategies

Students who are eager researchers learn quickly how to locate information in which they are interested, but if opportunities to practice their skills are not provided, students may soon forget what they have learned. Researching weekly provides ample opportunities for students to practice what they have learned while acquiring new skills in conjunction with new reference materials. For example, students in lower grades who are using a dictionary for the first time see that the words are alphabetized. This can carry over to using an encyclopedia, where the topics are alphabetized, and later to using an index in a reference book where the topics are alphabetized, and finally, to locating items in the autocat or on the shelf where the books are housed alphabetically by author's last name. Students in upper grades who are accustomed to using an encyclopedia to research a city, state, our county might be introduced to the specialized information found in atlases, almanacs, gazetteers, geographical dictionaries and so on.

How Brain Research Supports the Importance of Repeated Opportunities to Research

> "Guided sequential development ensures that students grasp the strategy and can internalize the process for application to research in many subject areas."
>
> *— Sharon Straathof, 1999, p. 139.*

In addition, neuroscientist Marian Diamond's research with rats at the University of California at Berkeley (Starr, 1999) found that rats which were provided with a larger amount of enrichment experiences at once became overstimulated and developed fewer changes in the cerebral cortex than did rats that experienced enrichment stimuli spread out over a period of time (p. 1). Applying this to the principal of repeated practice in research with InfoQuest, we can surmise that students will be more successful researchers if their efforts are spread out with repeated practice for an extended period rather than for an intensive but relatively short period of time, as in completing a research paper. Ken Haycock (2000) in his report "What Works," corroborates this finding by reporting that students typically need more time to "consume and absorb" the information they find than they are given (p. 1).

Bring attention to a variety of resources

Varying the types of research questions asked means that students would have a reason to seek information from a variety of sources. If every question could be answered in a dictionary, the students would tire of dictionary use quickly. But because a dictionary only provides one type of information, if the next question is the type that would be found in an almanac, for example, students begin to realize that there are different categories of reference materials and they are used for different types of information. With experience, students also become bolder in trying to locate information in different resources.

Encourage information seekers

Often all a student needs for encouragement is a word of recognition from an adult or one of their peers. In some schools, a weekly announcement listing the students who have correctly researched the question is an adequate reward, but sometimes the less motivated or less confident student needs more to continue researching. This is where the little prizes come in. Students enjoy receiving the little trinkets and begin to plan which ones they want to earn next, encouraging them to continue researching. Asking for student input into the prizes is effective too, if interest wanes. In addition, the little prizes become an opportunity for community resources to support the school. A variety of stores openly support learning projects in the schools and provide various donations to keep the program running. In our area, Target, Kroger and Chick Fil-A have been very supportive.

> "Generally students were unaware of the range of sources of information that could be used to identify relevant information; they had a poor understanding of the 'information landscape.'"
>
> — *Mark Hepworth, 1999, p. 6.*

How InfoQuest Meets These Criteria

InfoQuest meets all of the criteria listed above and more. It appeals to students of all ages and ability levels. It is quick and easy to implement. It requires little more than support from the classroom teachers but can be used to supplement any unit of study in any grade level. InfoQuest works with existing media resources but can be used to acquire funding for new and improved resources. Best of all, InfoQuest can be an on-going information literacy program which provides repeated access to resources and continues to build information literacy skills over an extended period of time, rather than for the duration of one research project. Read on to find out more about implementing your very own InfoQuest program.

> "Give frequent, early, positive feedback that supports students' beliefs that they can do well."
>
> — *Barbara Gross Davis, 1999, p. 1.*

Chapter 5

How to Ask H.O.T. Questions

A current buzzword in educational circles the last few years has been metacognition. Simply put, metacognition is the process of thinking about thinking. It involves reflection on the processes which actively engage the mind when learning occurs. If a student can reflect on, or monitor, his or her conscious thoughts when engaged in a discovery, creative thought, realization, idea, etc., the student can develop some control over the process.

> "If we want students to metacogitate, they must have daily practice."
> — *Virginia Rankin, 1999, p. 44.*

According to Julie Gordon (1996), students who have learned metacognition exhibit the following behaviors:

■ Planning: establishing goals

■ Strategizing: deciding on a method for achieving set goals

■ Knowing: learning what resources are needed

■ Monitoring: self-checking on progress

■ Evaluating: determining when goals are achieved

■ Terminating: ending task when goals are achieved (p. 2).

The student who can thus identify the activity, setting, thoughts, procedures, strategies, and other related factors that occur while learning is taking place can thereby ensure that learning will continue to occur. Learners who can monitor their own learning are more successful at critical thinking skills and problem solving.

Why Critical Thinking Skills Are So Important

Why is critical thinking so important? Critical thinkers are those who don't just memorize facts or regurgitate what has been taught to them. Critical thinkers can examine situations for similarities and differences, can derive new ideas from old, can probe persistently for a discovery. Our society needs critical thinkers to discover cures for diseases, to invent new and improved modes of transportation, to design safer buildings, to move civilization forward in art, science, technology, government, and more. Consider the following characteristics of critical thinkers:

| Figure 5.1 | *Characteristics of Critical Thinkers* |

Inquisitiveness	Flexibility	Curiosity
Alertness	Diligence	Balance
Persistence	Reflection	Originality
Risk-taking	Precision	Metacognition
Innovation	Divergence	Nonconformity

All of the above characteristics are noteworthy in individuals who possess them, but why are these specific characteristics important to society as a whole? Individuals who possess the above characteristics, who are, in short, critical thinkers, have been shown to be better problem solvers, and thus more productive employees and citizens of our society. Critical thinking skills are not only important for our students to excel in school and achieve a good education in preparation for the workplace, but critical thinking skills are also important for producing informed citizens. Being a critical thinker enables one to make thoughtful, informed decisions, to consider both sides of an issue, to reason, judge, rationalize. Without such skills, our society is endangered.

How to develop critical thinking skills

In 1956, Benjamin Bloom constructed a taxonomy of thinking skills that identified six levels of cognitive processing: knowledge, comprehension, application, analysis, synthesis, and evaluation (pp. 201–207). Experts generally agree that the first three levels of thinking in Bloom's taxonomy identify what is known as lower order thinking skills, while the last three levels identify higher order thinking, or H.O.T., skills.

> **"Knowing how to ask the right questions may be the single most important step in learning."**
> — *Christina Doyle, 1999, p. 99.*

Teachers who consistently ask recall-type questions that require a simple answer do not motivate students to develop higher order thinking skills. Student should be encouraged to think, consider, analyze, and wonder before answering a question. Questions that require more than one step to answer take students through a process of evaluating information in order to reach a conclusion. Consider the following sets of questions and the different nature of answers to each.

What was the Speedwell? Describe it.

Compare and contrast the Speedwell and the Mayflower.

What does absolute zero mean, in your own words?

Can you design some situations where absolute zero would be more important than 0° Fahrenheit?

What are the primary characteristics attributed to a sachem?

Consider the similarities and differences in a sachem and a guru. Why would Mahatma Gandhi be considered a guru?

Note that the first question in each set is straightforward and requires a simple, objective answer. The first question is easily researchable and a generic answer should be expected. In other words, each students' answer, while unique to that student, should be very similar. The second question in each set, however, is open to interpretation and is more subjective in nature. A range of answers could be considered acceptable, depending on the angle the student pursues in answering.

> **"Essential questions spark our curiosity and sense of wonder."**
> — *Jamie McKenzie, 1996, p. 1.*

The first question in each set corresponds with the lower order of Bloom's taxonomy: Question 1, "What is the Speedwell? Describe it," is a knowledge question; Question 3, "What does absolute zero mean, in your own words?" is a comprehension question; Question 5, "What are the primary characteristics attributed to a sachem?" is an application question. The second question in each set corresponds with the higher order of Bloom's taxonomy: Question 2, "Compare and contrast the Speedwell and the Mayflower," is an analysis question, Question 4, "Can you design some situations where absolute zero would be more important than 0° Fahrenheit?" is a synthesis question, and Question 6, "Consider the similarities and differences in a sachem and a guru. Why would Mahatma Gandhi be considered a guru?" is an evaluation question. Lower cognitive levels of questions are those which require a recall, direct, knowledge, factual answer. Higher cognitive questions are those which are open-ended, analytical, inferential, judgmental. While all levels of questions have their place in teaching information literacy skills, it is the higher order of questions which also promote critical thinking skills.

Good Beginnings

> "The process that is conducted in order to find answers to the right questions leads to a point at which information becomes knowledge."
>
> — *Christina Doyle, 1999, p. 99-100.*

In order for questions to promote higher order thinking, they must first have the right beginning. Generally speaking, questions that begin with the 5 W's (who, what, when, where, why) or H (how) by themselves are of the lower order of questions. Look again at the first question in each pair above. These questions began with "what…," which demands a simple, more objective type of answer. This level of questions is perfectly suited to students at the preliminary or beginning levels or research. Students at initial levels of research ability need to experience success frequently and should not be hindered by questions that require multi-tasking to answer. Straightforward questions which can be answered easily while research skills are quite appropriate for beginners. Such questions can certainly have their place in stimulating a desire to know and can be valuable in encouraging students to become familiar with the varieties of resources available for research. It is easy to develop lower levels of questions for trivia games and quiz shows. But you will not find such questions challenging to experts in higher order thinking! Higher order questions require more than one step or process, and cannot be answered without reflection on all points surrounding an issue. These H.O.T. questions often contain words such as the following:

■ What are some problems caused by…

■ What is most likely to happen if…

■ What might be the results of…

■ What factors most likely influenced…

■ What are the differences between…

- What are the similarities between…

- What could be produced with…

- What is your opinion of…

- What debate issue might affect the…

- How could the groups be organized differently in…

- What caused the…

Figure 5.2	*Characteristics of Good Questions*

The question must provoke thought, curiosity, and wonder
The question must be researchable
The question must have real-life application

A well-written question for InfoQuest should meet three criteria:

First, the question must provoke thought, curiosity, and wonder. It must pique a student's interest in a subject, and stimulate his mind to demand a response or a desire to know. Such a question can be based on a curious event, a funny name, an oddity in the natural world, the unexplained. It should be based on something that is outside the realm of common knowledge, something that is not widely known, but once asked, the student should realize the value of knowing the answer to such a question. Common topics include questions on Bigfoot, the Loch Ness Monster, the Bermuda Triangle, extraterrestrial life, Black Holes, supersonic travel, extinct creatures, and other such curiosities. Once the question is asked, students are curious to know the answer.

Second, the question must be researchable. It cannot be on a topic so obscure that students cannot locate information about it in a variety of sources. It must be popular enough to warrant coverage in magazine articles, newspaper articles, Web sites, encyclopedias, nonfiction books, CDs, and more. Students should not encounter too much discouragement in attempting to locate an answer. Moreover, the school library media specialist should determine ahead of time that any question asked can be answered through resources available at the school.

Third, the question should have a real-life application. The topic should be something students have little knowledge about but want to know more once they learn the question. If the question has a connection to the curriculum, it is even more desirable and motivating for students to research the answer, as the knowledge will benefit the student.

How Ineffective Questions Affect Students

How often have you encountered students who have been sent to the school library media center to "find out something" about a particular topic? For generations, teachers have assigned research topics without designing the specific questions students should answer or the angle to approach in their research. So, the students check an encyclopedia, the Internet, and perhaps a book or two for information on their topic. They gather up everything they can easily find and present it in their projects, regardless of the pertinence of the information. As a result, students find themselves trying to cover a topic that is too broad or too narrow, or flounder in determining whether the information they do locate is essential or insignificant to the purpose at hand.

> "Without strong questioning skills, you are just a passenger on someone else's tour bus. You may be on the right highway, but someone else is doing the driving."
>
> — *Jamie McKenzie, 1997, p. 1.*

No wonder students often find research tedious and unmotivating! Who would not be frustrated at a hit-or-miss proposal that is heavily weighted in terms of academic performance? Students who attempt to research a topic without specific criteria defined by a well-written question waste time, become frustrated, and fail to learn the essential skill of probing deeply into a topic. They also fail to learn how to ask the right types of questions themselves. Questioning is an essential research skill that students can only learn by dealing with well-written questions frequently enough to be able to identify the characteristics of a well-written question.

Teachers and media specialists can design questions so that all can succeed using the cognitive levels outlined in Bloom's taxonomy. Students who are working at the preliminary or beginning stages of research need to work with questions that are mainly lower order questions. Nevertheless, when these students become confident and well-informed on a specific topic, they may be further challenged by some higher-order levels of questions. At the same time, students who are intermediate or advanced might approach a subject with which they have a limited amount of knowledge by answering lower order questions initially. Then, as they become more knowledgeable, they can advance to higher order levels of questions. Students benefit most from a full range of questions, including some lower order and some higher order levels of questions.

The following model of Bloom's taxonomy provides a framework for developing questions which stimulate students to research, motivate them to probe deeply, ensure that critical thinking skills develop, and assist students in learning questioning skills themselves.

Figure 5.3	*Interpretation of Bloom's Taxonomy*	

Category	Student Behavior	Examples
Knowledge	Recalling facts, concepts	Which one What does it mean Select those which Recite from memory Create a timeline Identify the following
Comprehension	Understanding the meaning	Give examples In your own words Make a graph Demonstrate Summarize
Application	Using knowledge to solve Problems	Compute Solve Modify Construct a model Illustrate Show
Analysis	Breaking down material into Related parts	Compare Contrast Examine Investigate Separate Categorize
Synthesis	Produce something new From component parts	Invent Create Compose Devise Develop Predict Plan
Evaluation	Making a judgment after Thoroughly considering all	Debate Verify Justify Argue Recommend Assess Determine

In an age where information is multiplying more rapidly than we can master it, our students must learn to develop skills for learning, understanding, applying, analyzing, synthesizing, and evaluating information to determine what is most suitable for the need at hand. Questioning is an essential tool that, once mastered, will ensure our students become critical thinkers and efficient consumers of information. Models of superior questions will provide our students with the best examples for assimilating these skills.

Questioning is the key that unlocks the door to wonder. Research carries the students through that door and into different rooms in the house of knowledge.

Chapter *6*

How to Teach InfoQuest in the School Library Media Center or Classroom

InfoQuest is a game of challenging library research questions designed to teach information literacy skills. It provides repeated practice, progressive development, a variety of levels, and is easily adaptable to the school library media center or the classroom. If administered from the school library media center, it is most successful as a school-wide program. The program, however, is flexible enough to allow for adaptations to numerous teaching situations including self-contained classrooms, home-schooling, and more.

> **"The hallmark of a critical thinker is an inquiring mind."**
> — *A. King, 1994, p. 13.*

The following procedure explains how to administer the program school-wide:

Establish a set of questions to use each week. When I first began the program, I spent a few weeks over the summer collecting interesting questions and recording the answer for each as well as the source and page number for future reference. I typed out the questions in large, bold print, and mounted them on colorful construction paper strips, one question per strip. These strips were then laminated and spiral-bound into a flip book which I randomly flipped open to a different question each week. (Suggested questions follow in Chapters 7–15).

If your school year lasts the standard 190 days, and you wish to ask one question per week, you will need to prepare 38 questions (or about 40 questions with a couple of extra questions allowed as a safeguard). Questions can be theme-oriented or on a variety of subjects and levels, but they should

> "Ideally, effective library and information skills instruction not only helps students acquire the skills they need to be able to solve their information problems, but also stimulates and encourages intellectual curiosity, information-seeking, and exploration behaviors."
>
> — *Ruth V. Small, 1999, P. 1.*

be varied so that students will be exposed to a number of different resources in researching the answers. If this is your first program of this sort, begin with some intriguing but relatively easy questions to allow for student success. Work up to the more difficult questions as the program progresses.

At the first of each week, two previously-selected student volunteers announce the InfoQuest question of the week on the intercom during the morning announcements. The idea of this announcement is to grab the students' attention much like a television game show host would, using the following dialog:

InfoQuest Intercom Dialog

Speaker #1: Hello, boys and girls, and welcome to InfoQuest—the game of challenging library research questions!

In a moment, we will be asking this week's question, but before we do, let me remind you that you must answer the question in the school library media center between Monday and Thursday to receive credit and earn a prize. Anytime the media center is open before, during, or after school, or when your work is finished, ask your teacher if you can go to the school library media center to participate in InfoQuest.

And, now, here's our host for the week, _____.

Speaker #2: Hello, all you InfoQuest fans and welcome to this week's game. You will have all week to find the answer to the question using research materials in our school library media center. In order to win a prize, you must fill out the InfoQuest form and have the Media Specialist sign it after you find the answer.

And now, for this week's question. Are you ready? This week's question is: "Did Benjamin Franklin sign the Declaration of Independence?" Repeating, "Did Benjamin Franklin sign the Declaration of Independence?"

Procedure

■ Once the question has been announced, the students have the rest of the week to come to the media center to research the answer.

■ As students enter the media center, they sign a log book, indicating that they will abide by the rules, and pick up an InfoQuest answer form.

■ Rules for playing InfoQuest are prominently posted in the media center near the InfoQuest answer forms.

■ Answer forms must be filled out completely and legibly in order to receive credit. Illegible or incomplete forms are not accepted.

■ Students must submit their answer form to the media specialist or an assistant for checking and a signature validating the form.

■ The media specialist or an assistant will watch the InfoQuest participants to insure that the students actually do research the question in the media center and don't just simply write down an answer or otherwise cheat.

■ The media specialist or an assistant will give directions, hints, or answer questions as needed to assist less competent students in being successful.

■ The media specialist or an assistant will collect the completed forms and hold them until prizes are dispersed. (By holding the forms until we dispersed prizes, we were able to avoid problems with cheating.)

Figure 6.1   *Rules for Playing InfoQuest*

- ■ InfoQuest must be answered during the day in the school library media center.

- ■ Only one entry per student per week.

- ■ Students may receive assistance from the Media Specialist, an assistant, or a library aide.

- ■ No answers from outside sources will be accepted.

- ■ InfoQuest must be answered by the student in person, not by another student for a classmate.

- ■ If a student is unable to submit a written answer (student has an arm in a cast, for example), he/she may give it orally with the approval of the media specialist.

- ■ Students then fill out the following InfoQuest form with their name and home-room, the question they are researching, and the answer.

| Figure 6.2 | *InfoQuest Answer Forms* |

InfoQuest

Name _____

Homeroom _____

Question _____

Answer _____

Signed _____

InfoQuest

Name _____

Homeroom _____

Question _____

Answer _____

Signed _____

InfoQuest

Name _____

Homeroom _____

Question _____

Answer _____

Signed _____

InfoQuest

Name _____

Homeroom _____

Question _____

Answer _____

Signed _____

Tallying Forms and Recognizing Correct Responses

Students submit the completed form to a library media specialist or an assistant who signs it to indicate that the student actually researched the question in the media center. Completed forms are then placed in a box.

At the end of the week, all of the forms are tallied and sorted by classes. If space permits, this might be done as students submit forms. They simply place their form in the right box according to grade or homeroom. We found that forms could be tallied on a running spreadsheet as submitted, in much the same way that a student checks out a book, saving a lot of work at the end of the week.

Awards for correct responses are distributed to the students in each class who have answered correctly. The students can be announced on the intercom or can be recognized when they next come to the media center. If classes are on a fixed schedule, distributing awards by class schedule might be less disruptive. We tried operating both ways.

Awards can be tangible or intangible. We found that our younger students preferred to receive a small prize or token, but middle and upper grade students were happy to have their name announced or posted in a prominent place.

Included below is a list of both tangible and intangible awards. As a school library media specialist or classroom teacher, you should be the best judge of what is most appropriate for the students in your own school.

InfoQuest Awards

Tangible prizes awarded for InfoQuest can be inexpensive trinkets from a source such as the Oriental Trading Company, Party City, Really Good Stuff or other similar sources. Since it was somewhat controversial, individually wrapped candy was approved by our administration for upper grades only. No gum was allowed.

By presenting an overview of the InfoQuest program to our Parents' Association, we not only received their overwhelming support, but we also received funding to purchase prizes from the onset. Informing our parents of what was happening weekly, encouraged family involvement as they asked their children what the question of the week was and whether or not they had been into the media center to research the answer. This built a support base at home from the onset and helped InfoQuest become wildly popular from the beginning. So much interest was generated by the program that parents often came by to find the answer themselves—especially when they didn't believe the answers their children told them at home were correct!

It was very obvious from the beginning which prizes were most popular with the students, but it was also effective to ask them what they most looked forward to earning. Students were eager to respond and then eager to participate in hopes of being awarded the prize they had suggested.

Figure 6.3	Popular Prizes Given Throughout the Year	
Toy cars	Clickers	Jelly rings
Key chains	Stickers	Martian fingers
Party favors	Pencils	Parachute men
Shaped erasers	Tops	Assorted wrapped candy
Plastic animals	Eraser tops	Metallic rings
Plastic bugs	Yo-yos	Plastic figures

Intangible Awards

Our experience proved that students in the upper grades (5–8) were most frequently motivated by intangible rewards. The following is a list of awards which motivated our upper grades students to participate in InfoQuest: Certificates, Homework passes, Lunch passes, Computer time, Names posted on wall, Names announced on intercom, Special privileges, Being the next InfoQuest announcer, Seating awards, Assistant time, Student Mentors, Leadership awards, Names in the newsletter, Recognition from the principal.

InfoQuest provides many "teachable moments" where information skills can be taught in-depth. For example, the organization of knowledge according to the Dewey Decimal System is an appropriate lesson for the students who do not know where to begin searching for the answer to a question.

Figure 6.4	*Dewey Decimal System*
000-099	Generalities (Computers, Controversies, Journalism)
100-199	Philosophy/Psychology (Supernatural, Emotions, Ethics)
200-299	Religion/Mythology (Bible, World Religions, Mythology)
300-399	Social Sciences (Politics, Government, Economics)
400-499	Languages (Etymology, Sign Language, Foreign Language)
500-599	Natural Sciences (Math, Astronomy, Plant/Animal Kingdom)
600-699	Technology (Health, Medicine, Transportation)
700-799	Arts (Drawing, Music, Sports)
800-899	Literature (Plays, Shakespeare, Classics)
900-999	History/Geography (Exploration, Ancient History, World Events)

Troubleshooting

Even with the best-made plans, problems can arise. Here are some of the problems I encountered implementing InfoQuest and how I solved them:

Scenario No. 1: A group of younger children are fighting over who can use "the book" to find the answer.

    Suggestion: Set a limit of one or two students at a time using a resource and allow a five or 10 minute time limit so others can have a turn quickly. Have a variety of resources readily available that can be used for researching the answer. Prepare the materials in advance (Friday before) and have them set up for Monday's question.

Scenario No. 2: The younger children are writing in the expensive reference books!

    Suggestion: Have students place a clear sheet of Mylar (from a report cover) over the pages they are using to write down the answer. The Mylar can mark their place as well as protect the pages.

Scenario No. 3: The students change classes all day long and have no time to come to the media center.

    Suggestion: Have the media center open before and after school and during lunch and recess for such students. Allow them to use the resources when it fits into their schedule.

Scenario No. 4: The teachers only allow the same students each week to come to the media center.

    Suggestion: Ask students who are familiar with the process to bring a friend with them the next time they come. Work with counselors, resource teachers, and others to prepare a list of students who are not regular visitors to the media center but who might benefit from recognition. Seek out these students in the halls, lunchroom, etc. and address them specifically, saying something like, "I'll be looking for you next week, John."

Scenario No. 5: The teachers are not supportive.

    Suggestion: Win over the teachers gradually. Ask them what units they will be studying. Try to tie in research questions with their units of study to make a trip to the media center worthwhile for all of their students.

Scenario No. 6: The school library media center does not have enough current dictionaries (atlases, encyclopedias) to initiate an InfoQuest program.

    Suggestion: We were alarmed to find that our school library media center was lacking in many more areas than I realized before I began InfoQuest at our school. I began to compile of list of needs and sought funding to acquire them.

Scenario No. 7: The expensive reference materials are getting heavy use and even abuse. Pages are torn, covers and bindings torn, books dropped and pages dog-eared.

Suggestion: It was with dismay that I observed the expensive new reference materials getting heavy and destructive use. However, it was easier to approach groups for funding when I could vouch for the fact that a book had an average shelf life of 3–5 years and had evidence to support it. Showing the heavily used books was somewhat pleasing — it indicated our media center was a busy center of learning!

Modifications

InfoQuest is easily adapted from a school library media center activity to a unique activity designed to suit specific needs in individual classrooms.

■ InfoQuest can be used in classrooms by individual teachers.

Suggestions: Announce the week's question each Monday after the pledge of allegiance and morning announcements. Have a corner set up as the InfoQuest corner, with forms, pencils, master list of questions and reference material, or set up in the class library.

■ InfoQuest can be used as a bonus question for units of study.

Suggestions: Complete units with questions for further study which can earn bonus points for students who research the answers. Use as a weekly incentive or as independent study.

■ InfoQuest can be used for enrichment.

Suggestions: Keep advanced students and quick workers busy while slower ones finish assignments.

■ InfoQuest can be used as a center activity.

Suggestions: Set up as a flip book of questions in a center and change questions weekly.

■ InfoQuest questions can be posted on the chalkboard weekly for extra credit assignments.

Suggestions: give willing students the opportunity to explore the public library on their own or surf the net for extra credit.

■ InfoQuest can be assigned as homework.

Suggestions: Give a weekly InfoQuest question as a homework assignment.

Stages in Teaching Research Skills Using InfoQuest

Stage I Preliminary Researchers

Students who are preliminary researchers can be guided through the research process with an oral walk-through:

Example: What is the question you must answer this week? Can you read it to me?

What is the main word (or words) in that question? This book might be helpful in finding the answer to that question. We can use the index to tell us where to look in the book. The index lists key words in alphabetical order. This book has an article on bats (or whatever the subject of the question is) on page 21. Let's turn to page 21 and see if we can answer the question now.

Stage II Beginning Researchers

(Students who are beginning researchers should already be familiar with some of the research process such as using the catalog to locate a source, using a table of contents, and so on.) Students who are independent readers can be guided in the research process with specific questions or hints as to where the question might be answered.

Example: What is the question you must answer this week? What is the main word (or words) in this question? Can you think of a place to look for information on that subject? Have you tried looking in the dictionary (encyclopedia, gazetteer, almanac, etc.) for information on that subject?

Stage III Intermediate Researchers

Student who are already familiar with the research process can be guided with general hints as to where the question might be answered:

Example: What is the question you must answer this week? What is the main word (or words) in that question? Where have you tried looking for information on this subject? Some places you might look are (list three possibilities with the correct one among them)

Stage IV Advanced Researchers

Advanced researchers should be able to work independently with an occasional directive or suggestion.

Fund Raising with InfoQuest

Initiating a program such as InfoQuest can attract new attention to your media center. My own experience with the program showed increased patronage from the onset. As students become interested in and challenged by the questions, they began to find more and more reasons to come to the media center — some on a regular basis, and some almost daily. The ones who came regularly answered nearly every question asked. The students who came more often brought their friends and classmates in to answer the questions, sometimes acting as mentors to show others how to fill in the forms and how to search for the answer. Their visits often extended beyond answering the question, and they began to peruse the collection for items of special interest to them.

Teachers began to note the increased enthusiasm and "jumped on the bandwagon" by requesting special materials for projects, bringing in classes more frequently, or simply searching for the answer themselves. Some teachers even began to browse, picking up a magazine or two, or bringing in lesson plans and asking me for suggestions for resources. This renewed interest led to additional opportunities to collaborate, even to the point of coordinating the InfoQuest questions with current areas of study in the classrooms.

Parents also showed an interest, and many came in just to see what all the fuss was about. They had heard the weekly InfoQuest questions discussed at home, and often came to find the answers for themselves, especially if the correct answer surprised them.

While all this attention can be a very positive experience, it also calls attention to the size and scope of your school library media center collection. As patronage increases, so do requests for materials—often revealing materials that are outdated or of poor quality. When this happened to me, I used the opportunity to reveal gaps in the collection and to stage a fund-raising campaign to fill them.

Once I identified the needs in our collection, our Parents' Association pledged $16,500 to purchase 1,000 new books for research. This amount assumed an average cost of $16.50 per book. Of course, many books cost much more than that, particularly reference books. Since the program required a heavy use of reference materials in addition to high-quality nonfiction books, and, since many of our reference materials were outdated, I realized that much more money was needed. With the assistance of some wonderful parent volunteers, we began fund-raising in earnest.

Some of the fund-raising activities at our school included bake sales, fall festivals, garage sales, auctions, book fairs, car washes, wrapping paper sales, walk-a-thons, a fun run, and a talent show.

InfoQuest is a road map to the journey of inquiry. How far you venture down that road is your choice, but the journey is new every time you travel.

Chapter 7

Getting Started with InfoQuest

One of the most exciting parts of general research is that odd bits of trivia can be fascinating. So much trivia abounds that television game shows such as *Hollywood Squares, Jeopardy, Who Wants to be a Millionaire?* and so on have developed a popular following from trivia fans. One good way to introduce students to research is with just such a game. General sources of information such as a good student dictionary, a student thesaurus, an encyclopedia (print or electronic), an almanac, a yearbook, and so forth are excellent tools for research games. My experience has shown that students frequently respond well to a trivia scavenger hunt or some other reference game as an introduction to research. Several such reference games are described in this chapter.

Information Literacy Skills Associated with General Research

Research with general reference sources is closely related to a variety of skills from the skills continuum introduced in Chapter 3. Also, general research lends itself well to a variety or organizational and presentation formats including spreadsheets, charts, graphs, tables, timelines, multimedia presentations, oral presentations, and more. The possibilities are as varied as the range of information. Some of the organizing and presenting skills (from all levels) associated with general research include:

- Putting events in proper order

- Summarizing important details

- Selecting a topic sentence

- Using graphic organizers for search results

- Utilizing outline for search results

- Utilizing word processing, spreadsheet, database, and other software programs to format and organize information

- Using graphic programs to illustrate information and create charts, graphs, tables

- Recognizing bias, irrelevant statements, suitability of resource

- Utilizing note cards

- Compiling bibliographical information

- Correctly formatting citations

- Paraphrasing correctly

- Retelling information in own words

- Participating in a group discussion on information learned

- Preparing a newscast, speech, or other oral presentation of information

- Writing information in editorial, newsletter, report, etc.

- Visually displaying information in poster, videotape, slide show, chart, graph, table, multimedia presentation, and so on

- Supporting all points with authoritative statistics

Questions and Answers on General Research

Not only are general sources of information a great way to compile interesting questions, but they are also of wide appeal to all ages. After students become adept at researching, they may begin to suggest research questions of their own, or whole classes can develop research questions around a thematic unit of study. Student-authored questions frequently attract attention to areas of research that adults may overlook but to which students are naturally drawn. Examples of subjects which naturally interest children are the supernatural, the unexplained, the record-breakers and record-setters, the animal world, especially the unusual, rare, or endangered species, and so on. Whole classes can devote time to skimming research materials and developing research questions of their own. This process is empowering to students, makes them feel confident and helps develop familiarity with a variety of research materials. The student-authored questions are among the most popular questions we have posed for InfoQuest, especially when the author of the question is announced with the question.

The following sets of questions are not ability-grouped (Preliminary, Beginning, Intermediate, Advanced) as are the questions in the remaining chapters. Rather, the following questions are designed for use as an introduction to research, as an initial InfoQuest program, or as part of a research game such as a library media center scavenger hunt, a reference race, a research jeopardy game, or a Reference bingo game, an almanac adventure, and so on. The type of game depends on the interests of the students and varies from school to school, but the applications are endless. Directions for the games mentioned using InfoQuest questions are at the end of this chapter. Additional suggestions for individualizing your InfoQuest program include:

■ using InfoQuest questions as boardwork either, daily or weekly, or as needed

■ creating learning centers with InfoQuest questions and research materials

■ using InfoQuest questions as bonus, extra-credit or challenge work for high-ability students

■ assigning InfoQuest questions for homework, teamwork, groupwork, or as assuagements on which students can work with mentors

■ using InfoQuest questions for Internet research challenges and more

■ hosting a library media center scavenger hunt

The opportunities abound and vary from situation to situation.

The following is the original list of InfoQuest questions as published in *Library Talk* Magazine in the 1999 January/February issue. This list was the source of the weekly general reference question used school-wide at the time. Such a list is an excellent way to begin an InfoQuest program in your own school.

Original InfoQuest *Questions*

1. What is the last word in the Declaration of Independence?

2. Which amendment to the constitution gave 18-year-olds the right to vote?

3. What does DTP stand for?

4. What was Christopher Carson's nickname?

5. What pen name did Emily Bronte use?

6. What is an erg?

7. What is a tufa?

8. Name 3 legumes.

9. What part of a spider is a protein?

10. Who was Rachel Carson?

11. What is unusual about a male seahorse?

12. Which creature is larger, a sperm whale or a giant squid?

13. What is a female fox called?

14. Which cats are bigger — tigers or lions?

15. What is the smallest mammal?

16. Why do glowworms glow?

17. Which bird has the most feathers?

18. Who has more bones — a child or an adult?

19. What was ENIAC?

20. What and where is the Globe Theater?

21. What is a stupa?

22. What is a mermaid's purse?

23. What nocturnal animal lives in a sett?

24. Which famous bicycle race takes place in France each year?

25. Where did a black widow spider get its name?

26. If an earthquake occurs at the bottom of the ocean, what happens?

27. Who is Kim Campbell?

28. Who is D.W. Griffith?

29. In what year did Lucille Ball of "I Love Lucy" die?

30. What type of dinosaur is a dacentrurus and where were its bones found?

31. What did valdosaurus dinosaurs eat — plants or animals?

32. The well-known writer, Arthur Miller published 2 plays in 1991. What were they?

33. James Dickey, the poet and novelist, was born in what city?

34. Did Lewis Sinclair ever win a Nobel Prize for literature?

35. Isaac Singer, the well-known American writer, was born in Poland. Where and when did he die?

36. Who wrote the poem, The Bells?

37. How much should you tip a strolling musician in a nice restaurant?

38. Who (in the Bible) is Methuselah and how long did he live?

39. Where was the first mortuary?

40. In what reference book other than an encyclopedia can you find a biography of Edgar Allen Poe?

41. Who said, "Cognito ergo sum"?

42. Where is Bora Bora?

43. Who said "Live and let live"?

1. What is the last word in the Declaration of Independence? **Honor**

2. Which amendment to the constitution gave 18-year-olds the right to vote? **26th**

3. What does DTP stand for? **Desk top publishing**

4. What was Christopher Carson's nickname? **Kit Carson**

5. What pen name did Emily Bronte use? **Ellis Bell**

6. What is an erg? **Unit for measuring work or energy**

7. What is a tufa? **A powdery rock**

8. Name 3 legumes. **Peas, beans, soybeans**

9. What part of a spider is a protein? **Liquid used to spin a web**

10. Who was Rachel Carson? **Environmentalist and author of Silent Spring**

11. What is unusual about a male seahorse? **The male has a pouch for babies**

12. Which creature is larger, a sperm whale or a giant squid? **Sperm whale**

13. What is a female fox called? **Vixen**

14. Which cats are bigger — tigers or lions? **Tigers**

15. What is the smallest mammal? **Kittis hog-nosed bat**

16. Why do glowworms glow? **To attract a mate**

17. Which bird has the most feathers? **A tundra swan**

18. Who has more bones — a child or an adult? **A child**

19. What was ENIAC? (Acronym for Electronic Numerical Integrator and Computer) **The first computer**

20. What and where is the Globe Theater? **Shakespeare's plays were performed there, England**

21. What is a stupa? **A Buddhist temple**

22. What is a mermaid's purse? **A skate ray lays flattened eggs in a leathery pouch, which, when empty washes onto shore and is known as a mermaid's purse**

23. What nocturnal animal lives in a sett? **A badger**

24. Which famous bicycle race takes place in France each year? **Tour de France**

25. Where did a black widow spider get its name? **The female kills its mate**

26. If an earthquake occurs at the bottom of the ocean, what happens? **A tsunami**

27. Who is Kim Campbell? **The first female Prime Minister of Canada**

28. Who is D.W. Griffith? **A famous filmmaker**

29. In what year did Lucille Ball of *I Love Lucy* die? **1989**

30. What type of dinosaur is a dacentrurus and where were its bones found? **It is a stegosaurus and bones were found in England, Portugal, and France**

31. What did valdosaurus dinosaurs eat — plants or animals? **Plants**

32. The well-known writer, Arthur Miller published 2 plays in 1991. What were they? **"Ride Down Mt. Morgan" and "The Last Yankee"**

33. James Dickey, the poet and novelist, was born in what city? **Atlanta**

34. Did Lewis Sinclair ever win a Nobel Prize for literature? **Yes, in 1930**

35. Isaac Singer, the well-known American writer, was born in Poland. Where and when did he die? **1991 in Miami**

36. Who wrote the poem, "The Bells"? **Edgar Allen Poe**

37. How much should you tip a strolling musician in a nice restaurant? **Answers may vary, but $1 to $5 is customary**

38. Who (in the Bible) is Methuselah and how long did he live? **Longest living person ever recorded-the Bible records his life at 969 years**

39. Where was the first mortuary? **Collingwood Memorial in Toledo, Ohio which opened Sept. 15, 1930**

40. In what reference book other than an encyclopedia can you find a biography of Edgar Allen Poe? **Answers may vary, depending on the library collection**

41. Who said, "Cognito ergo sum"? **Thomas Carew (1595–1639) wrote "I think therefore I am" in Le Discours de la Methode (1617)**

42. Where is Bora Bora? **Bora Bora is a Polynesian island in the South Pacific**

43. Who said "Live and let live"? **this is an old Scottish proverb**

Games Using InfoQuest Questions

Reference Jeopardy

An excellent way to introduce your older but not-so-research savvy students to research is to play a game such as Reference Jeopardy. As you may know, the television version of *Jeopardy* is played with a three-dimensional gameboard that lists multiple categories worth increasing increments from $200 up to $1000. The game begins with a player who selects a category and value (i.e., Natural World for $200) from which to begin play. Underneath the category and value square is the answer to a question. All of the players have an opportunity to buzz in with the question that matches that answer. The correct selection wins that amount of money for the player.

Playing Reference Jeopardy is very similar, but I find that it helps to give my students a head start by supplying them with the questions in advance. They then have a period of time (such as three to five class periods or whatever is reasonable) to research the questions themselves in preparation for the game. The questions number more than the number of questions used in the game and cover at least five subject areas such as math, science, history, geography, literature, biography, sports, art, music, etc. The original InfoQuest questions at the beginning of this chapter work well for this purpose, or additional questions on specific subjects (coming in later chapters) can be used as well.

In the meantime, I make a gameboard out of poster paper, marking off sections with a ruler and labeling these sections with subject categories (Science, History, Biography, etc.). I make the gameboard reusable by sticking on answer squares which can be removed later. (Rubber cement works well here.) On top of these answer squares I place sticky notes with the increment levels from 200 to 1,000. The subject categories are permanent as they can be used repeatedly.

We divide the group into teams with a representative player from each team who is designated to answer the question for the team. Each team is supplied with a desktop bell (available at office supply stores for less than $5).

The game is played with a toss to determine which team selects the beginning category and question level. After that, any team may attempt to answer the question. The first team ringing the bell will be given the opportunity to answer.

A correct answer scores the selected number of points for a team. An incorrect answer subtracts that amount of point from the team's score. If a team answers incorrectly, the other team(s) may attempt to answer. The game ends when all of the answers on the gameboard are exhausted. (An additional round requires another gameboard and additional questions.)

The students work quite hard to answer the questions and remember the answers when they know these will be used for a game such as this. It is quite effective in introducing students to a wide variety of reference materials, particularly students who are accustomed to using only encyclopedias or the Internet for research. It also encourages teamwork and collaboration and is an excellent extension of a class unit of study.

| Figure 7.1 | Reference Jeopardy Gameboard Model |

200	200	200	200	200
400	400	400	400	400
600	600	600	600	600
800	800	800	800	800
1000	1000	1000	1000	1000

Reference Tic-Tac-Toe

This game is similar to the Reference Jeopardy game above but is best used after a semester of playing InfoQuest in a classroom or schoolwide.

Divide the class into two teams. Each team will select a team leader who will answer the question for the team.

The emcee will ask an InfoQuest question (which has been previously researched) and the player must correctly answer the question in order to put a mark on a board. If a team answers incorrectly, the mark goes to the other team unless the mark is to win the game. At that point, the other team must correctly answer the question in order to win the mark. The first team to get a series of Xs or Os in a vertical, horizontal, or diagonal line wins the game.

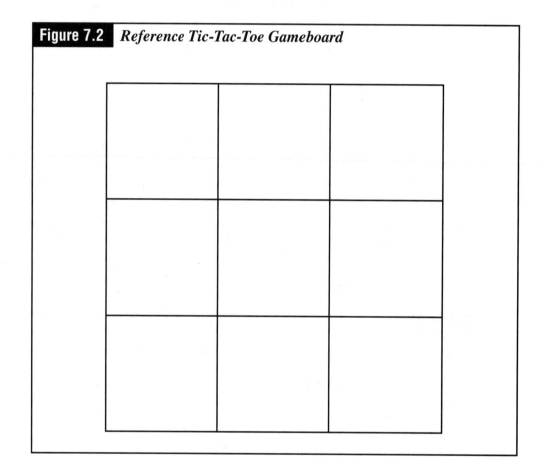

Figure 7.2 *Reference Tic-Tac-Toe Gameboard*

Reference Race

This game is played in small groups or in teams of two. Each team receives a printout of the Reference Race gameboard and a stack of question cards. The stacks of cards contain an equivalent number of questions which are similar in nature and difficulty but are unique to that team (to prevent cheating). Questions can be subject-specific (such as the questions that follow in the next few chapters) or a variety such as those used for Reference Jeopardy. Each team must fill in the squares on the gameboard with the keyword(s) in the question as well as the answer and the source where the answer was located. The first team to correctly complete the gameboard wins the game. (Keep answers for each team's question cards handy for quick checking.)

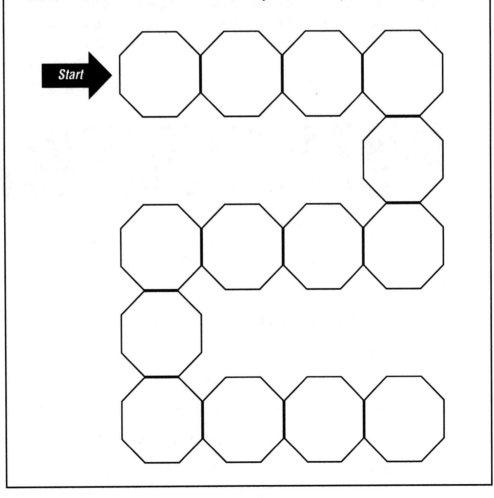

Figure 7.3 | *Reference Race Gameboard*

Reference Race

Read each question on your question cards carefully. In each space on the gameboard, write in the keyword of the question, the answer, and the source where the answer was located. The first team to correctly fill in all the spaces wins the game.

Start

Almanac Adventure

This game is played individually or in teams of two or three. Students must use an almanac or some other similar quick reference book of facts to answer the questions. The first team to answer all questions correctly wins the game. This sort of competition encourages students to concentrate on using their skills efficiently and to divide the labor in order to work quickly. It discourages web surfing and ogling over pictures in reference books as there is a time limit to their research. Students can usually complete the 20 questions in one 40-minute class period. If class periods are longer or shorter, adjust the number of questions accordingly.

Before initiating the Almanac Adventure, give students a brief introduction to the types of information found in an almanac or yearbook. Display several almanacs, such as the *World Almanac and Book of Facts* and *The Information Please Almanac*, and several yearbooks such as the *Guinness Book of World Records* and the *Guinness Sports Records Book*. Demonstrate how the index is used in each to locate a fact quickly. Share some of the types of information found in each. Ask a sample question or two and ask a volunteer to suggest the best source for locating the answer to that question.

It may be helpful to students to explain that almanacs, yearbooks, and many quick reference books are often kept near the reference desk for quick reference. Librarians often refer to these to answer patron questions. Samples of quick reference books such as *Famous First Facts, The Book of Lists, The New York Times Desk Reference*, and so on should be available for students to examine. Share some of the types of information available in each.

Almanac Adventure — *Questions*

Using the *World Almanac and Book of Facts, The Information Please Almanac*, or the *Guinness Book of World Records* (or other similar quick reference books of facts), find the answers to the following:

1. What is the world's largest animal?

2. What is the largest insect?

3. What is the fastest animal in the world?

4. Which zoo in the United States has the most species of animals?

5. Which is the longest tunnel in the world and where is it?

6. How many countries are currently in the world?

7. Where is the Mona Lisa exhibited today?

8. What is the average amount of water each American uses today?

Almanac Adventure

9. How many kinds of beetles are there?

10. Who and where is the oldest living person?

11. How many times a day does the human heart beat?

12. How many muscles do you have in your body?

13. Do you use more muscles to frown or to smile?

14. When was the bicycle invented and by whom?

15. Who was the first person to go around the world and when?

16. What is the record for the largest hamburger ever eaten?

17. Who was the first woman senator?

18. Where was the first post office?

19. Where was the first motion picture theater?

20. What are the most valuable animals owned by people?

Almanac Adventure *Answers*

1. What is the world's largest animal? **Blue whale**

2. What is the largest insect? **Atlas moth**

3. What is the fastest insect in the world? **dragonfly**

4. Which zoo in the United States has the most species of animals? **San Diego Zoo**

5. Which is the longest tunnel in the world and where is it? **NYC West Delaware water supply tunnel in Yonkers, NY**

6. How many countries are currently in the world? **192**

7. Where is the Mona Lisa exhibited today? **The Louvre, Paris, France**

8. What is the average amount of water each American uses today? **123 gallons**

9. How many kinds of beetles are there? **290,000**

10. Who and where did the person with the longest recorded lifespan live? **Jeanne Louise Calumet of France**

11. How many times a day does the human heart beat? **100,000**

12. How many muscles do you have in your body? **More than 650**

13. Do you use more muscles to frown or to smile? **frown**

14. When was the bicycle invented and by whom? **Kirkpatrick MacMillan in 1839**

15. Who was the first person to go around the world and when? **Elizabeth Cochrane in 1889–90 took 72 hours to go around the world alone**

16. What is the record for the largest hamburger ever eaten? **21 feet/5,520 pounds**

17. Who was the first woman senator? **Rebecca Latimer Felton, a Democrat, was appointed to the Senate by the governor of Georgia on Oct. 3, 1922 to fill a vacancy caused by the death of Senator Thomas Edward Watson**

18. Where was the first post office? **Boston, Massachusetts**

19. Where was the first motion picture theater? **The Electric Theater in Los Angeles, California opened in 1902 as the first motion picture theater**

20. What are the most valuable animals owned by people? **Racehorses**

Scavenger Hunt

A scavenger hunt is an exciting way for students to become familiar with the variety of materials offered in the media center. Have students work in small groups or pairs. Distribute a set of questions to each group or pair. For best results, vary the questions slightly for each group or pair. (Make sure question sets are of comparable difficulty and subject matter.) Students should determine the keyword in each questions to begin searching. Use a variety of questions that cover a number of different subject areas. Questions used for the Reference Race or Reference Jeopardy or the two sets of InfoQuest questions found in this chapter work well for this scavenger hunt, but unlike the Reference Jeopardy, do not allow the students to look up the answers ahead of time. Instead, the students should be seeing the questions for the first time in this scavenger hunt.

Resources For Preparing Your Own General Reference InfoQuest Questions

Ardley, Bridget and Neil Ardley. (1989). *Random House Book of 1001 Questions and Answers*. New York: Random House.

Asimov, Isaac. (1981). *Isaac Asimov's Book of Facts*. New York: Bell Publishing.

Fantastic Book of 1000 Lists. (1999). New York: Dorling Kindersley.

Farndon, John. (1993). *Eyewitness Question and Answer Book*. New York: Dorling Kindersley.

Fascinating Facts About Nature, Science, Space, and Much More! (1998). Courage Books.

Guinness World Records. (2000) Mint Publishing.

I Wonder Why Encyclopedia. (1997) New York: Kingfisher Books.

Kane, Joseph Nathan, et al. (1997). *Famous First Facts 5th ed*. New York: H.W. Wilson.

Kids' Question and Answer Book from the Editors of Owl Magazine. (1987). New York: Grosset and Dunlap.

Kranes, Marsha. (1999). *5087 Trivia Questions and Answers*. Black Dog and Leventhal Publishers.

Louis, David. *2201 Fascinating Facts*. (1983). The Ridge Press and Crown Publishers.

Pansini, Anna. *Kids' Question and Answer Book*. (1991). Mahwah, NJ: Troll Associates.

Wallechinsky, David, and Irving Wallace. (1978). *People's Almanac*. William Morrow.

World Almanac and Book of Facts 2000. (1999). World Almanac.

World Almanac for Kids. (1999). World Almanac.

Chapter 8

Wondering About Words

Comprehending words and their subtle differences in meaning, communicating clearly, and explaining ideas thoughtfully are skills too often inadequate in even our best-educated students. Facility with words and application of word skills begin with a working knowledge of the dictionary and thesaurus.

> "I still find the English dictionary the most interesting book in our language."
>
> —*Albert Jay Nock*

Today there are picture dictionaries, unabridged dictionaries, multilingual dictionaries, the *Oxford English Dictionary*—a whole range of dictionaries for every skill level and every purpose. Students should have a variety of dictionaries available and be aware of the benefits of each kind.

Thesauri are almost as numerous as dictionaries. They vary from the traditional indexed arrangement to alphabetical listings. Also of interest are special dictionaries such as *Brewer's Dictionary of Phrase and Fable, Webster's Etymological Dictionary,* Bible dictionaries, and dictionaries of foreign words and phrases in English. Some popular titles of dictionaries and thesauri are listed at the end of this chapter.

Information Literacy Skills Associated with Research On Words and Their Origins

Word research is slightly different from research in other subject areas. The information gathered from word research, while interesting and informative, does not lend itself to as many modes of presentation as does other research. Instead, word research is usually a component of some other project. Nevertheless, a number of the information literacy skills noted in the skills continuum in Chapter 3 are related to word research.

Questions and Answers on Words and Their Origins

The following sets of questions on all four levels are designed to help students develop facility with the standard English dictionary, special dictionaries, and the thesaurus. The questions focus on foreign words and phrases, word origins, words that appear to be related but are not, and food words that have interesting histories. The questions can be used one at a time, such as a weekly question from the school library media center, or as bonus questions in the classroom, or all together as a special research project. The use is up to the individual classroom teacher or school library media specialist—whatever works best in her situation.

Word Wizard
Preliminary

Questions

The following questions were designed to assist you in becoming familiar with the dictionary. Pay particular attention to the italicized words. Look them up first, then answer the question.

1. What is a *bolero* and who might use it?

2. In which country would you need a *cicerone*?

3. Where would you be most likely to find a *mahout*?

4. What would you do for a broken *tibia*?

5. Where could you find a *bayou*?

6. Do you have a *babushka*? What is another word for *babushka*?

7. Who might use a *boutonniere*?

8. What is a *boycott* and how was it named?

9. When would you need an *armada*?

10. What is the best way to be *frugal*?

1. A **bolero** is a short jacket such as a bullfighter might wear.

2. You might need a **cicerone**, or tour guide, in Italy.

3. You would probably find a **mahout**, or elephant driver, in India.

4. A broken **tibia** would require a cast on your leg.

5. A wet swamp, or **bayou**, can be found in lowlands such as coastal Louisiana, Georgia, Florida, and South Carolina.

6. If you have a grandmother, you have a **babushka**.

7. An usher, bridegroom, or prom escort should wear a **boutonniere**.

8. A **boycott** is a refusal to use the services of a business in order to protest. It originated when Irish tenants ostracized Charles Boycott (1832–1897), land agent in County Mayo, because he refused to lower their rents.

9. You might need an **armada**, or fleet of ships, in a war.

10. The best way to be **frugal** is not to spend any money. Save it!

Research the following italicized words to find out the origin, or history, of each food's name.

1. Where did *melba toast* get its name?

2. Where is *couscous* served and what is it?

3. Where would *chateaubriand* most likely be served?

4. How did *Graham crackers* get their name?

5. What are *hors d'oeuvres* and where might you eat them?

6. What are *bruschetta* and where did they originate?

7. What is *brie*?

8. Who might serve *polenta* with *gorgonzola*?

9. When is *sorbet* offered?

10. What is the history of *sandwiches*?

I'll Eat My Words
Preliminary

1. **Melba** toast (and peach **melba**) is named for Dame Nellie Melba (1861–1931), a famous Australian soprano.

2. **Couscous**, a pasta product made from crushed semolina grain, is popular in the Middle East.

3. A fine restaurant might serve **chateaubriand**, a prime center cut of beef tenderloin stuffed with seasonings before grilling.

4. A health-conscious American vegetarian who urged dietary reform, Sylvester **Graham** (1894–1951), introduced these crackers made from whole wheat flour.

5. **Hors d'oeuvres** is French for appetizers (literally "outside of work," or "extra"); you might have them at a party.

6. **Bruschetta** are pieces of crusty bread grilled in oil and topped with tomatoes, spices, and cheese. The dish originated in Italy.

7. **Brie** is soft French cheese.

8. **Polenta**, a side dish made of boiled corn meal with **gorgonzola** cheese, is often served in Italy.

9. **Sorbet**, the frozen fruit dessert, is offered after a meal.

10. The Earl of Sandwich (1718–1792) placed his meat between two slices of bread so he would not have to interrupt his gambling for a meal, thus inventing the **sandwich**.

The following questions are designed to help you distinguish between words. Search for the keywords in each question in order to begin researching the answer. Determine what the question is asking of you. Avoid unrelated information in your response.

1. Compare and contrast a brioche and a brooch.

2. Would you prefer a baguette or a brilliant diamond? Why?

3. Who might use a nosegay and why?

4. At a funeral, would you be more likely to find a Eucharist or a eulogist? Why?

5. If you think someone else's work would be a model for others, would you say it is exemplary or worth emulating? Why?

6. What is the difference between an ayah and a nannie?

7. Would an abigail be more closely related to a nursemaid or a chambermaid? Explain.

8. If you were an archer, would you be most interested in a bowyer or a bowler? Why?

9. Would you see a cordivainer or a cadaver to repair a shoe? Explain the difference.

10. Aside from spelling, what is the difference between a jehu and a yahoo?

1. A brioche is a soft, light-textured yeast bread; a brooch is a large ornamental pin.

2. A baguette is a rectangular faceted cut diamond, while a brilliant is the traditional round faceted cut. It's a matter of individual choice.

3. A nosegay was a wrist corsage of flowers that was held close to the nose to mask unpleasant odors.

4. Liturgical church funeral services often include the Eucharist (mass, communion, or Lord's supper), but all funerals, wherever they are held, have a eulogist, a speaker who recalls the deceased with praise and affection.

5. If someone else's work is held up a model for others, it is both exemplary (held up as an example) and worth emulating (copying).

6. The only difference in the two is the country of origin. An ayah in India is the same as a nannie in England. Both are entrusted with the care of the children in a household.

7. An abigail would be more closely related to a nursemaid, who is a caretaker or domestic servant employed in a specific family; a chambermaid cleans bedroom suites or hotel rooms and usually has little or no relationship with the occupants of the suite.

8. An archer would be most interested in a bowyer, who makes or sells bows for archers, while a bowler, who plays cricket or bowls, would be of little interest.

9. A cordivainer is a shoe repairman, while a cadaver is a body, such as medical students might use in their studies.

10. A jehu is a chariot driver in the Middle East, while a yahoo is a derogatory term used to describe a crude or boorish individual.

What Do You Mean?

Read the following questions carefully. Find meanings of keywords in a dictionary, thesaurus, special subject dictionary, etymological dictionary, or dictionary of foreign words and phrases.

1. Would a matched ensemble be worth more than separates?

2. Who might have just cause to act in a clandestine fashion?

3. If your hostess served an insipid tea, would you ask for seconds?

4. Where might you find an ornate frieze?

5. Would it be appropriate to open a meeting with a maxim?

6. Mores dictated that a feast be held on the full moon. How many syllables in mores?

7. Would you have reason to fear a nemesis? What is the word's origin?

8. Give a familiar example of meeting protocol.

9. Whose name is synonymous with opprobrium? Why?

10. If you were a patient, would it be better to be ambulatory? Why?

11. Might a woolly mammoth be a hirsute specimen? Name another hirsute creature.

12. Could a colloquial form be appealing?

13. Who might need a femme de chambre?

14. What is Grimm's law and when did it originate?

15. What is xerophthalmia and what causes it?

16. What is a mattock and who would need one?

17. What does YHWH stand for?

18. What is the significance of Maundy Thursday?

19. If you were served a bombe, would you eat it? Why?

20. What is the historical significance of being of Aryan descent?

1. A matched ensemble might be a designer outfit; it costs more than separates that might or might not match with other items.

2. A spy might need to act in a clandestine, or secretive, fashion.

3. It is unlikely that a guest would ask for seconds of an insipid, or tasteless, tea.

4. You might find an ornate frieze, or decorative carving, in an expensive dwelling, a public building, a church or an historic building.

5. A maxim, or witty saying, is often used to catch the audience's attention in opening a meeting or beginning a speech.

6. *Mores,* or customs, has two syllables.

7. The Greek word nemesis means downfall and generally instills fear.

8. Any procedure from Robert's Rules of Order, such as making a motion requiring a second, would be an example of meeting protocol.

9. President Nixon is a name synonymous with opprobrium as he is the only President of the United States to resign for inappropriate behavior following the Watergate affair. (Opprobrium means disgrace; accept any justified name related with disgrace such as this one. Other examples could be Clinton because of his affairs or scandals, Prince Charles for the same reason, etc.)

10. An ambulatory patient can move around, which is preferable to being bedridden.

11. A woolly mammoth would definitely be a hirsute, or hairy, specimen. A monkey is another.

12. A colloquial, or local, form of speech might appeal to some; it also reveal the region in which the speaker was raised.

13. A femme de chambre is often employed by the wealthy to clean bedrooms.

14. Grimm's law is a formula that explains how sounds in one language are changed in another language with a similar base.

15. Xerophthalmia is an eye disease caused by a lack of Vitamin A.

16. A farmer, gardener, or woodcutter might use a mattock, a digging tool with the blade set at right angles to the handle.

17. YHWH is transliterated as Jehovah, the proper Hebrew name for God.

18. Maundy Thursday was the day Jesus partook of the Last Supper with the twelve apostles.

19. A bombe is a frozen ice cream dessert, usually layered and round in shape. Yes, I would eat it!

20. World War II was fought to a great extent over Hitler's belief that Aryans, or gentile Caucasians, were the superior race.

Now that you have found the definitions for the 20 terms above, see if you can decipher the message below and rewrite it to be more easily understood:

Beware the femme de chambre dressed in a black and white ensemble. On Maundy

Beware the chambermaid dressed in a black and white outfit. On the Thursday before Easter,

Thursday, she served her mistress an insipid green broth. The following day, she was

she served her mistress a tasteless tea. The next day, she was suspiciously

surreptitiously lingering near the frieze. In similar circumstances, mores dictate that she

hanging around the decorative band that runs around the wall. It would be customary to

be fired for her clandestine affairs, but her semi-ambulatory Aryan mistress who suffers

fire her for her secretive behavior, but her invalid Caucasian gentile mistress, who is

from xerophthalmia, broke all protocol by giving her a warning and a raise. When a

nearly blind, didn't act as expected and gave her a warning and a raise. When a

needle was found in the bombe last evening and the femme de chambre was found with a

needle was found in the frozen dessert last night and the chambermaid was found with an

mattock in her hand, the police took her into custody. Her attorney said something about

ax in her hand, the police took her into custody. Her attorney said something about

claiming Grimm's law. Only YHWH knows whether she is guilty of attempted murder or

a language barrier. Only God knows whether she is guilty of attempted murder or

not, but now we fear her nemesis. At any rate, her name will be forever synonymous with

not, but now we fear her downfall. At any rate, her name has been associated with

opprobrium. No maxim by a witty attorney can change what she had planned.

misconduct. No attorney's witty sayings can change what she had planned.

Resources for Planning Your Own InfoQuest Program on Words:

Adeleye, Gabriel G. *World Dictionary of Foreign Expressions.* (1999). Wauconda, Illinois: Bolchazy-Carducci.

The American Heritage Children's Dictionary. (1998). Boston: Houghton Mifflin.

The American Heritage Picture Dictionary. (1998). Boston: Houghton Mifflin.

The American Heritage High School Dictionary. (1993). Boston: Houghton Mifflin.

Borman, Jami Llynne. *Computer Dictionary for Kids—and Their Parents.* (1995). Hauppage, NY: Barron's.

Brewer, Ebenezer Cobham. *Brewer's Dictionary of Phrase and Fable*. (1981). London: Cassell.

Chambers Dictionary of Etymology. (1988). NY: Chambers Harrap Publishers, Inc.

Concise Dictionary of English Etymology. (1988). NY: Oxford University Press.

DK Merriam Webster's Children's Dictionary, 1ST American Edition. (2000). NY: Dorling Kindersley.

Guthrie, Richard L. *Children's Bible Dictionary*. (1998). Hauppage, NY: Barron's Educational Series.

Hellweg, Paul, Joyce LeBaron, and Susannah LeBaron. (1999). *The American Heritage Student Thesaurus*. Boston: Houghton Mifflin.

Hendrickson, Robert. *Encyclopedia of Word and Phrase Origins*. (1987). NY: Facts on File.

Lincoln Writing Dictionary for Children. (1988). NY: Harcourt Brace Jovanovich.

Morris, William and Mary. (1987). *Morris Dictionary of Word and Phrase Origins*. NY: Facts on File.

Oxford Dictionary of Foreign Words and Phrases. (1997). NY: Oxford University Press.

Seuss, Dr. *Cat in the Hat Dictionary*. NY: Beginner Books, 1964.

Urdang, Laurence. *Oxford Thesaurus* (American Edition). NY: Oxford University Press, 1992.

Whiting, Bartlett Jere. *Modern Proverbs and Proverbial Sayings*. Cambridge, MA: Harvard University Press, 1992.

Wittels, Harriet, and Joan Greisman. *The Clear and Simple Thesaurus Dictionary*. NY: Grossett and Dunlap, 1996.

Wiersma, Debbie Butcher. *Precious Moments Children's Bible Dictionary*. Grand Rapids, MI: Baker Books, 1994.

Chapter 9

Musing on Mathematics

Mathematics, one of the oldest fields of study, is
continually expanding. From the ancient school at
Alexandria, founded in 300 B.C., until modern times, the
study of mathematics has fascinated great minds around the
world.

> **"We now know that under appropriate conditions, virtually all students can learn significant amounts of arithmetic, algebra, geometry, statistics, functions, and trigonometry..."**
>
> *— Zalman Usiskin*
> *(1993, p. 8)*

Throughout history, mathematical computation has
been assisted with mechanical devices from rocks and
sticks to the abacus to calculating devices, many of which
were the forerunners of modern computers. Most children
are fascinated by computers today but know little of the
history behind the computer as we know it. This subject
can be intriguing for computer buffs to research.
Measurements have an interesting history, as well; many
measurements are derived from body parts. In my experience, even the most
reluctant math students have been drawn in to math by projects involving
measurement. Today, both young and old alike delight in math mysteries and
are intrigued with problem solving. Some of these subjects are covered in the
questions in this chapter.

Information Literacy Skills Related to Math Research

Some of the information literacy skills associated with mathematical research include

- Restating a question in one's own words

- Identifying the keyword

- Formulating a list of related topics

- Recognizing sources that fit specific search criteria

- Using an index, table of contents, headings, subheadings

- Paraphrasing information

- Comparing information from various sources

- Summarizing information

- Writing notes

- Outlining

- Narrowing or broadening a topic

- Using charts, graphs, tables to organize and present information

- Identifying irrelevant statements

- Distinguishing between fact and opinion

- Retelling information in one's own words

- Boolean search strategies

- Classifying and organizing information

- Logical sorting

- Determining validity

- Identifying contradictions in statements

- Graphic organizers

- Charts, graphs, tables

- Ability to benefit from computer programs such as spreadsheets

Questions and Answers on Mathematical Research

The following sets of questions on all four levels are designed to help students expand their knowledge of mathematics and mathematicians and inspire them to delve deeper into this challenging and intriguing field. Questions cover measurements, the metric system, mathematicians, computer history, and some thought-provoking tidbits from the history of mathematics. Resources for planning your own InfoQuest math program are listed at the end of the chapter.

Math Matters!
Preliminary

Questions

The following questions are designed to help you develop knowledge of units of measurement and how they are used. Look up the italicized keyword(s) first and then answer the question.

1. What is the unit of measure for the *speed of a ship?*

2. What is the unit of measure for *500 sheets of paper?*

3. What is the unit of measure for the *intensity of sound?*

4. What is the unit of measure for *light energy?*

5. What is the unit of measure for the *power used to propel weight forward?*

6. What is the name of the *diameter of a gun bore?*

7. What is the name for the *speed of a computer processor?*

8. What is the name of *speed at which a vehicle travels faster than the speed of sound?*

9. *Energy* is measured in what unit?

10. What is the unit of measure for *electrical current?*

Math Matters!
Preliminary

1. What is the unit of measure for the speed of a ship? **knots**

2. What is the unit of measure for 500 sheets of paper? **ream**

3. What is the unit of measure for the intensity of sound? **decibel**

4. What is the unit of measure for light energy? **watt**

5. What is the unit of measure for the power used to propel weight forward? **horsepower**

6. What is the name of the diameter of a gun bore? **caliber**

7. What is the name for the speed of a computer processor? **Megaherz or gigaherz**

8. What is the name of speed at which a vehicle travels faster than the speed of sound? **mach**

9. Energy is measured in what unit? **erg**

10. What is the unit of measure for electrical current? **amp**

How Does it Compute?

Questions

The following questions are designed to acquaint you with those individuals who and those instruments which have made a significant contribution to the field of mathematics.

1. Who was *Howard Aiken* and for what was he known?

2. *John Von Neumann* wrote a book on quantum theory at age 28. What else did he contribute to the field of mathematics?

3. For what was *Vannevar Bush* best known?

4. Who was *Charles Babbage* and what was his contribution?

5. *Norbert Wiener* developed cybernetics. What is it?

6. What is a *suan pan?* How is it significant?

7. *Lord William Thomson Kelvin* invented the Kelvin scale for measuring absolute temperature. For what else was he known?

8. What is the history of the *abacus*?

1. Who was Howard Aiken and for what was he known? **Howard Aiken was a Harvard professor who built the first digital computer.**

2. John Von Neumann wrote a book on quantum theory at age 28. What else did he contribute to the field of mathematics? **John von Neumann built one of the first electronic computers.**

3. For what was Vannevar Bush best known? **Vannevar Bush built the first analog computer in 1931.**

4. Who was Charles Babbage and what was his contribution? **Babbage developed a difference engine for calculating logarithms to 20 decimals and an analytic engine similar to a modern computer.**

5. Norbert Wiener developed cybernetics. What is it? **Cybernetics is the belief that many thought processes in the brain could be adapted to machines. This belief paved the way for the artificial intelligence concept of today's computers.**

6. What is a suan pan? How is it significant? **A suan pan is a Chinese abacus. The abacus was the first calculating machine.**

7. Lord William Thomson Kelvin invented the Kelvin scale for measuring absolute temperature. For what else was he known? **Lord Kelvin built a Kelvin machine which was used in predicting high and low tides and was a forerunner to the modern computer.**

8. What is the history of the abacus? **Answers may vary but should include the idea that this was the first device man created to assist in calculating.**

1. Compare and contrast the name for the purity of gold versus the weight of a precious stone.

2. What unit of measure is closely related to the British standard for measurement of weight? How do they compare?

3. How much is a pennyweight? When is a pennyweight used?

4. Which is the smallest amount: dram, ounce, pint, milliliter? How do you know?

5. Twenty hundredweight is equivalent to what measure? When is twenty hundredweight used and why?

6. One mile is how many furlongs? When are furlongs used in place of miles?

7. Which is greater—40 rods or 1/4 mile? How do you know?

8. Which is greater—a meter or a yard? Explain your answer.

9. Which is greater—a gallon or a liter? How do you know?

10. Which is greater—a pound or a kilogram? Explain your answer.

11. Which is greater—a centimeter or an inch?

12. One fathom is equivalent to how many feet? When is a fathom used instead of feet?

13. One hogshead in equal to what other measure? When would a hoghead be used?

1. Compare and contrast the name for the purity of gold versus the weight of a precious stone. **Karat vs. carat.**

2. What unit of measure is closely related to the British standard for measurement of weight? How do they compare? **Pounds vs. kilograms; 1 kilogram is about 2 pounds.**

3. How much is a pennyweight? When is a pennyweight used? **1/20 of an ounce = 1 pennyweight; pennyweights are used in troy weight measures, where 1 lb=12 oz.**

4. Which is the smallest amount: dram, ounce, pint, milliliter? How do you know? **Milliliter; 8 drams=1 ounce; 16 ounces = 1 pint; one milliliter is 1/1000 of a liter.**

5. Twenty hundredweight is equivalent to what measure? When is twenty hundredweight used and why? **Twenty hundredweight = one ton, or twenty times one hundred pounds. Twenty hundredweight is used in heavy weight measurements.**

6. One mile is how many furlongs? When are furlongs used in place of miles? **8 furlongs = one mile. Furlongs are a linear measure like miles. Furlongs would be used in measures less than a mile.**

7. Which is greater—40 rods or 1/4 mile? How do you know? **One-quarter mile is greater. 40 rods=660 ft. and 1/4 mile= 1320 ft.**

8. Which is greater—a meter or a yard? Explain your answer. **A meter is approximately 39 inches while a yard is 36 inches, so a meter is greater.**

9. Which is greater—a gallon or a liter? How do you know? **A gallon is greater. One liter is about .264 gallons; a gallon is 3.785 liters.**

10. Which is greater—a pound or a kilogram? Explain your answer. **A kilogram is greater; one kilogram is about 2 pounds.**

11. Which is greater—a centimeter or an inch? *One inch.*

12. One fathom is equivalent to how many feet? When is a fathom used in place of feet? **6 feet; a fathom is used in nautical measures.**

13. One hogshead in equal to what other measure? When would a hogshead be used? **2 barrels; a hogshead is used in large liquid measures in the US.**

Math Marvels

Advanced

Questions

1. Negative numbers were used in China as early as 100 BC. The Hindus represented a negative balance with negative numbers in 700 AD. Can you devise a different way to represent negative values? Explain how you arrived at your answer.

2. In 1299, Italy forbade the use of anything other than Roman numerals for bankers. They thought that Hindu-Arabic numbers were more easily forged. What do you think? Do you agree? Should banks use Roman numerals to prevent forgery?

3. Why do you think so many famous mathematicians were men? Study the biographies of Maria Agnesi, Evelyn Granville, Hypatia of Alexandria and other women. What made these women successful in mathematics? Give examples in your answer.

4. In 1946, Eniac, the first electronic computer, was invented. It performed numerical calculations. Of course, today's computers perform many tasks besides calculating. What operations would you like a computer to perform? How do you think a computer could be programmed to perform them?

5. In 1960, the metric system was adopted by nearly every country in the world except the United States. Why do you think the United States is not using the metric system? What could be done to indoctrinate Americans with the metric system? Devise a plan to help America adopt the metric system. Explain how it works.

6. Algebra is the branch of mathematics that works with an unknown in an equation, and it has applications in everyday life. With algebra, travelers can determine if the amount of gas in the tank will need to be replaced before they reach their destination, businesses can determine when to replace aging equipment. What are some other applications of algebra in everyday life? Name several and explain why you selected those.

7. Eratosthenes calculated the distance around the earth based on the circumference of a circle and known distances between two points. Using Eratosthenes' calculations, Columbus could have determined that his journey would be 25,000 miles, but everyone dismissed those figures at the time. What do you think Columbus might have done if the distance had been proved to be correct?

8. Units of measure were originally derived from sizes of body parts. For example, Egyptians built the pyramids using parts of their arms as units of length, but since everyone's body parts were different, it was decided to use those of the pharoah as standard. The smallest unit was a digit—the width of one finger—and the cubit was the length from fingertips to elbow. Create a new system of measurement other than one based on body parts. Explain how you arrived at your units and why.

1. Negative numbers were used in China as early as 100 BC. …Can you devise a different way to represent negative values? **Accept all supported answers.**

2. In 1299, Italy forbade the use of anything other than Roman numerals for bankers. …Should banks use Roman numerals to prevent forgery? **Accept all supported answers.**

3. Why do you think so many famous mathematicians were men? Study the biographies of Maria Agnesi, Evelyn Granville, Hypatia of Alexandria and other women. **Nearly all of these women were brilliant as children, well educated, and appreciated for their skills.**

4. In 1946, Eniac, the first electronic computer, was invented. …What operations would you like a computer to perform? How do you think a computer could be programmed to perform them? **Answers may vary.**

5. In 1960, the metric system was adopted by nearly every country in the world except the United States. Why do you think the United States is not using the metric system? What could be done to indoctrinate Americans with the metric system? Devise a plan to help America adopt the metric system. Explain how it works. **Accept all supported answers. Most will probably include legal means of enforcing the metric system.**

6. Algebra is the branch of mathematics that works with an unknown in an equation, and it has applications in everyday life. …What are some other applications of algebra in everyday life? Name several and explain why you selected those. **Any application that involves an unknown quantity can be an example.**

7. Eratosthenes calculated the distance around the earth based on the circumference of a circle and known distances between two points. …What do you think Columbus might have done if the distance had been proved to be correct? **Answers may vary.**

8. Units of measure were originally derived from sizes of body parts. …Create a new system of measurement other than one based on body parts. Explain how you arrived at your units and why. **Answers may vary but should not be based on body parts.**

Resources for Preparing Your Own InfoQuest Math Program:

Bendick, Jeanne and Marcia Levin. (1965). *Mathematics illustrated dictionary*. NY: McGraw-Hill Book Company.

Bruno, Leonard C. (1999). *Math and mathematicians*. Detroit: U.X.L.

Weisstein, Eric W. (1995). *CRC concise encyclopedia of math*. NY: Chapman and Hall/CRC.

Chapter 10

Searching in Science

Children are naturally curious about the world around them. Often the first research experience a child has is with a science inquiry such as "Why is the sky blue?" or "Where does the sun go at night?"

The study of science includes biology, chemistry, physics, astronomy, zoology, botany, geology, and much more. Science subjects which students seem naturally drawn to include animals (zoology), particularly unusual animals, endangered animals, and prehistoric animals such as dinosaurs, the invisible world (chemistry), and the unexplained.

> "True science teaches, above all, to doubt and be ignorant."
>
> – *Miguel de Unamuno (Bartlett's Quotations, 1992, p. 589).*

Information Literacy Skills Related to Science Research

Nearly all skills in the skills continuum are related to science research but of particular interest are:

- Restating a question in one's own words

- Identifying the keyword

- Formulating a list of related topics

- Recognizing sources that fit specific search criteria

- Testing a theory

- Devising a philosophy based on personal beliefs supported with research

- Using an index, table of contents, headings, subheadings

- Paraphrasing information

- Comparing information from various sources

- Summarizing information

- Writing notes

- Outlining

- Narrowing or broadening a topic

- Using charts, graphs, tables to organize and present information

- Identifying irrelevant statements

- Distinguishing between fact and opinion

- Retelling information in one's own words

- Creating a newscast, speech, documentary, or other form of presentation

Questions and Answers on Science Research

This chapter includes questions on creepy critters, animal similarities and differences, the invisible world, and some thought-provoking ideas about the unexplained. Resources for creating your own sets of *InfoQuest* science questions are listed at the end of this chapter.

Creepy Critters

Preliminary

Read each question carefully. Use the keywords in italicized type to help you research the answer to each question.

1. What are the *fastest moving insects?*

2. What is the *heaviest insect?*

3. What is the *name of a jellyfish stinger?*

4. What are the most *ferocious freshwater fish?*

5. What separates *tarantulas* from other spiders?

6. Why don't other insects eat *ladybugs?*

7. Do *all lizards* have *legs?*

8. What is the *world's smallest mammal?*

9. How is a *fly* able to *walk upside down* on the ceiling?

10. How are *bats helpful to man?*

1. What are the fastest moving insects? **Large tropical cockroaches can move up to 3.35 mph or 50 times their length per second.**

2. What is the heaviest insect? **Goliath beetles of equatorial Africa grow up to 4.3 inches long and weigh 2–3 ounces.**

3. What is the name of a jellyfish stinger? **Jellyfish tentacles bear nematocysts, or cells that are responsible for their sting.**

4. What are the most ferocious freshwater fish? **Piranhas have razor-sharp teeth and will attack any injured or struggling creature, even humans.**

5. What separates tarantulas from other spiders? **Most tarantulas don't build webs.**

6. Why don't other insects eat ladybugs? **To other insects ladybugs look and taste terrible.**

7. Do all lizards have legs? **No, some lizards are legless like snakes.**

8. What is the world's smallest mammal? **The bumblebee bat of Thailand is the smallest mammal, weighing less than a penny.**

9. How is a fly able to walk upside down on the ceiling? **Flies have claws, pads, and a sticky substance on the bottoms of their feet, enabling them to walk upside down on the ceiling.**

10. How are bats helpful to man? **Bats help propogate plants and reduce the number of insects.**

Read each question below carefully. Use the keywords in italicized type to help you research the answer to each question.

1. Table salt is a harmless compound made of *two poisonous elements*. What are they?

2. All matter is made up of *molecules*. Molecules are made up of *atoms*. Atoms are made up of *particles*. What makes up particles?

3. What is another name for *splitting atomic nuclei?*

4. What is another name for *combining atomic nuclei?*

5. What is necessary for a *thermonuclear reaction?*

6. What common compound is a result of *electrovalent bonding?*

7. What common compound is a result of *covalent bonding?*

8. What is the force that holds *unlike molecules* together?

9. Rubber is a *natural polymer*. Are there any man-made polymers?

10. Murray Gell-Manor, the Cal-Tech physicist who discovered *quarks*, named them a after a famous *book by Joyce*. What was the name of that book?

11. How many *types of quarks* are there?

1. Table salt is a harmless compound made of two poisonous elements. What are they? **Chlorine and sodium.**

2. All matter is made up of molecules. Molecules are made up of atoms. Atoms are made up of particles. What makes up particles? **quarks**

3. What is another name for splitting atomic nuclei? **nuclear fission**

4. What is another name for combining atomic nuclei? **Nuclear fusion or a thermonuclear reaction**

5. What is necessary for a thermonuclear reaction? **Very high temperature in millions of degrees**

6. What common compound is a result of electrovalent bonding? **salt**

7. What common compound is a result of covalent bonding? **water**

8. What is the force that holds unlike molecules together? **cohesion**

9. Rubber is a natural polymer. Are there any man-made polymers? **Nylon, dacron, orlon, teflon, polyethylene, polystyrene**

10. Murray Gell-Manor, the Cal-Tech physicist who discovered quarks, named them a after a famous book by Joyce. What was the name of that book? *Finnegan's Wake*

10. How many types of quarks are there? **3**

Animania

Intermediate

Questions

Read the following questions carefully, noting the keywords and the specific information the question requires in its answer.

1. What is the difference between an alligator and a crocodile?

2. What is the difference between a frog and a toad?

3. What makes a yak a useful animal in the mountainous regions of Asia?

4. To what common housepet could a quoll be compared?

5. Compare and contrast a nombat and a wombat.

6. What characteristics of a sloth set it apart from other animals?

7. What is the difference between a horse and a pony?

8. Compare and contrast a woodchuck and a groundhog.

9. Compare a modern yak to a prehistoric woolly mammoth.

10. In what ways is the now extinct saber tooth tiger similar to a modern tiger? How is it different?

1. What is the difference between an alligator and a crocodile? **The crocodile is much more aggressive and has powerful jaws, and narrower snout and a tooth which is visible from the lower jaw even when the jaws are closed.**

2. What is the difference between a frog and a toad? **Frogs are slimmer with smoother skin; toads have dry, warty skin and emit a poison from their parotid glands.**

3. What makes a yak a useful animal in the mountainous regions of Asia? **Yaks are able to survive the bitter cold temperatures in the mountainous regions of Asia and are useful as pack animals, as well as for milk and milk products and clothing.**

4. To what common housepet could a quoll be compared? **A quoll is a maruspial which kills rodents, much like a housecat**

5. Compare and contrast a numbat and a wombat. **Both are marsupials and indigenous to the Australian forests, but a wombat is three times the size of a numbat and has hardly any tail; a numbat has no pouch; in fall, the wombat has one baby the numbat usually has a small liter in late winter or early spring; wombats can live up to 20 years**

6. What characteristics of a sloth set it apart from other animals? **A sloth's hair grows down not up, it has extra neck vertebrae, it drags rather than walks on limbs and has poor sight and hearing**

7. What is the difference between a horse and a pony? **A pony is a smaller breed of horse.**

8. Compare and contrast a woodchuck and a groundhog. **They are the same animal!**

9. Compare a modern yak to a prehistoric woolly mammoth. **Both have (had) habitats in the mountainous regions of Asia and were large in size, with woolly mammoths being larger than modern yaks; yaks are of the ox family and are easily domesticated and used as pack animals. Woolly mammoths seem to be more closely related to the modern elephant.**

10. In what ways is the now extinct saber-tooth tiger similar to a modern tiger? How is it different? **Both tigers are of the cat family, and were fierce hunters of approximately the same size and boasting a similar body structure. The saber-tooth had an extremely long canines which aided its killing its prey by stabbing and slashing its throat. Unlike the saber-tooth tiger, the modern tiger is endangered or becoming extinct because tigers have been hunted for their skins and bones.**

1. Why do you think UFOs have been reported worldwide but governments have dismissed the reports as bogus?

2. What is your opinion of the mystery of Flight 19 in the Bermuda Triangle? Why do you think the Bermuda Triangle continues to mystify us? What do you think might explain the disappearances there?

3. Do you think it is possible for a dinosaur-like sea creature to have survived since prehistoric times? How do you explain the Loch Ness monster? Do you think there is a relationship between the Loch Ness monster and a sea creature like the giant squid?

4. Research reports of the Beast of Gevaudan. For what was he known? How did he die? Do you think this story proves the existence of werewolves? Why or why not?

5. Many reports have documented ape-like creatures named Sasquatch, Bigfoot, the Abominable Snowman, and Yeti. Some dismiss these claims, saying the what was seen was simply a gorilla. Do you think these animals are gorillas? What do you think? Justify your answer.

6. Fantasy creatures like dragons, fairies, unicorns, leprechauns, and more have endured from generation to generation. Do you think they exist? Why or why not?

7. Can you find evidence that Atlantis was more than a myth and actually existed? Support your answer.

8. For centuries sailors at various times have reported spotting mermaids. Do you think these sightings were mirages? Scientist claim that these creatures must have been seals. What do you think?

Answers may vary as these questions are controversial with no documented scientific support but students should indicate research into the topic of each question and their answers should be supported with examples, reports, discussion.

Resources for Preparing Your Science InfoQuest Program:

Amazing animals of the world. (1995). Danbury, CT: Grolier Educational Corporation.

Burnham, Robert. (2000). *Readers' Digest Children's Atlas of the Universe*. Pleasantville, NY: Reader's Digest Children's Books.

Burnie, David. (1991). *How Nature Works*. Pleasantville, NY: Readers' Digest Association, Inc.

Grolier Students' Encyclopedia of Endangered Species. (1995). Danbury, CT: Grolier Educational Corporation.

The Guinness Book of World Records. (1999). NY: Facts on File.

Macmillan Encyclopedia of Science. (1997). New York: Macmillan Reference.

McGraw Hill Encyclopedia of Science and Technology. 6th ed. (1987). New York, NY: McGraw Hill Book Co.

The Raintree Illustrated Science Encyclopedia. (1992). Austin, TX: Steck-Vaughn Co.

Scientists: The Lives and Works of 150 Scientists. (1996). Detroit: U.X.L.

Strange and Unexplained Happenings. (1995). NY: Gale.

Van Nostrand's Science Encyclopedia. 6th ed. (1983). New York, New York: Van Nostran Reinhold Co.

The Way Nature Works. (1992). New York, NY: Macmillan Publishing Co., Inc

World Book's Young Scientist.(1995). Chicago: World Book, Inc.

Chapter 11

Queries on Quotations

A quotation is a memorable saying of another individual. Quotations may be derived from conversations, speeches, plays, essays, films, interviews, songs, even titles. Sometimes another person's words are quoted verbatim, but often just the main idea of a speaker is repeated. It is, however, the exact choices and combinations of another's words which make a phrase memorable. It is that exact choice and combination of words which communicates wit and wisdom, convention and culture, and has the power to initiate a change in thought or action in the listener. For this reason, quotations are an important part of a good education.

> "The quotations when engraved upon the memory give you good thoughts."
>
> *Sir Winston Churchill from* Roving Commission: My Early Life *(Bartlett's Quotations, 1992, p. 619).*

Information Literacy Skills Related to Quotation Research

Some information literacy skills which are related to the study of quotations include:

- Realizing that the school library media center and school library media specialist, books, magazines, newspapers, computer databases, software, and the Internet are sources of information or assistance with information

- Showing pleasure in visiting the library media center in supervised or unsupervised groups and individually

- Demonstrating responsibility in use of library media center materials

- Knowing how to correctly handle books, magazines, newspapers, computers, peripherals, and software, and audiovisual equipment

- Knows procedure for borrowing and returning a book, searching the catalog, searching other library catalogs and databases, putting materials on hold or on reserve, ordering materials through interlibrary loan

- Communicating what she wants to know

- Accurately formulating a question, theory, or philosophy

- Identifying the location of fiction, nonfiction, and reference books and other materials

- Recognizing that the catalog provides information about the author, title, illustrator, publisher, subject, related subjects, summary, bibliographical information

- Feels comfortable with the library media center staff

- Feels comfortable asking for or giving assistance

- Feels comfortable working independently or in a group

- Uses time purposefully in library media center without supervision

- Broadening or narrowing a topic

- Brainstorming related topics

- Realizing that print and nonprint sources serve different functions

- Realizing that the same source can vary in print and nonprint formats

- Realizing that sources of information can be primary or secondary

- Realizing that the best sources fit specific criteria

- Locating a subject in an encyclopedia

- Using an index and table of contents to find information in a specific resource

- Skimming and scanning for information

- Using a computer to locate, open, save, delete, move, and rename files and print documents

- Logging on the Internet and using a browser

- Using a search engine to perform a keyword search

- Using truncation, phraseology, parentheses, Boolean and other advanced search strategies

Questions and Answers on Quotation Research

This chapter includes some famous quotations from speeches, historic events, great literary works such as plays, short stories, poetry, novels, screenplays, even graffiti. Students will be asked to identify the speakers, occasions, and sources of the quotes, to compare similar thoughts and messages, or to draw conclusions about the speakers and/or quotations.

1. Who is known for saying, "I have a dream that one day my four little children…will not be judged by the color of their skin, but by the content of their character."?

2. "One small step for man, one giant leap for mankind" was spoken by whom and when?

3. "Ask not what your country can do for you; ask what you can do for your country" were famous words uttered by this beloved individual. Who said it?

4. "Never give in, never give in, never, never, never, never…" was in a speech delivered by this individual. Who said it and when?

5. "Toto, I've a feeling we're not in Kansas anymore" became the famous line of this individual. Who said it and when?

6. "To thine own self be true" is often quoted. What is the source of this quotation and who is being quoted?

7. "A house divided against itself cannot stand" were famous words uttered by this famous individual. Who said it and when?

8. "He that troubleth his own house shall inherit the wind." Name the source of this quote and the speaker.

9. "Two roads diverged in a wood and I—I took the one less traveled by, and that has made all the difference." This famous line can be credited to whom?

10. What is the source of the following poignant line: "In spite of everything, I still believe that people are really good at heart."?

1. Who is known for saying, "I have a dream that one day my four little children… will not be judged by the color of their skin, but by the content of their character."? **Martin Luther King, Jr. in a civil rights speech in Washington on Aug. 28, 1963.**

2. "One small step for man, one giant leap for mankind" was spoken by whom and when? **Neil Armstrong uttered these famous words when he became the first man to walk on the moon on July 20, 1969.**

3. "Ask not what your country can do for you; ask what you can do for your country" were famous words uttered by this beloved individual. Who said it? **John Fitzgerald Kennedy spoke these words in his inaugural address on January 20, 1961.**

4. "Never give in, never give in, never, never, never, never…" was in a speech delivered by this individual. Who said it and when? **Winston Churchill made this speech at Harrow School on Oct. 29, 1941.**

5. "Toto, I've a feeling we're not in Kansas anymore" became the famous line of this individual. Who said it and when? **Judy Garland made fame with this line from the screenplay to *The Wizard of Oz* in 1939.**

6. "To thine own self be true" is often quoted. What is the source of this quotation and who is being quoted? **This quotation is taken from William Shakespeare's *Hamlet*.**

7. "A house divided against itself cannot stand" were famous words uttered by this famous individual. Who said it and when? **Abraham Lincoln quoted this text from Mark 3:25 in a speech at the Republican Convention in Springfield, Illinois on June 16, 1858.**

8. "He that troubleth his own house shall inherit the wind." Name the source of this quote and the speaker. **This was spoken by King Solomon and is recorded in Proverbs 11:29.**

9. "Two roads diverged in a wood and I—I took the one less traveled by, and that has made all the difference." **This famous line can be credited to whom? Robert Frost from "The Road Not Taken" written in 1916.**

10. What is the source of the following poignant line: "In spite of everything, I still believe that people are really good at heart."? **These words were written by Anne Frank on July 15, 1944 in her diary which was later published as *The Diary of a Young Girl*.**

Who Said That?

Preliminary

Read each quotation below. Note the emphasized word. Look up the quotation and cite the author and some information about the quote such as date and/or source.

1. Eat to live and not live to eat.

2. It is the supreme art of the teacher to awaken joy in creative expression and knowledge.

3. O, death, where is thy sting?

4. A bird in the hand is worth two in the bush.

5. Do all the good you can,
   By all the means you can,
   In all the ways you can,
   In all the places you can,
   At all the times you can
   To all the people you can
   As long as ever you can.

6. I think that I shall never see
   A poem as lovely as a tree.

7. A teacher affects eternity. He can never tell where his influence stops.

8. Create in me a clean heart, O God; and renew a right spirit within me.

9. Go the the ant, thou sluggard; consider his ways, and be wise;

10. No man can serve two masters; for either he will hate the one, and love the other; or else he will hold to the one and despise the other. Ye cannot serve God and mammon.

10. Success is counted sweetest by those who ne'er succeed.

12. Genius is one percent inspiration and 99 percent perspiration.

13. I have nothing to offer but blood, toil, tears, and sweat.

14. To read well, that is, to read true books in a true spirit is a noble exercise.

15. I want to be alone.

16. The universe is wider than our views of it.

17. Sin has many tools, but a lie is the handle which fits them all.

18. You must train children to their studies in a playful manner....

19. Always do right—this will gratify some and astonish the rest.

20. Let not him who is houseless pull down the house of another.

21. If a man hasn't discovered something he will die for, he isn't fit to live.

22. Our destiny is bound up with the destiny of every other American.

23. Nothing you can do for children is ever wasted.

24. Kilroy was here.

25. We will now discuss in a little more detail the Struggle for Existence.

1. Eat to live and not live to eat. **Moliére, (1622–1673) in "The Miser" Act. 3, Scene 1.**

2. It is the supreme art of the teacher to awaken joy in creative expression and knowledge. **Albert Einstein (1879–1955), motto for astronomy building of Jr. College in Pasadena, California**

3. O, death, where is thy sting? **The Apostle Paul in 1 Corinthians 15:55.**

4. A bird in the hand is worth two in the bush. **Old English proverb quoted in several sources**

5. Do all the good you can,
   By all the means you can,
   In all the ways you can,
   In all the places you can,
   At all the times you can
   To all the people you can
   As long as ever you can.
   This quotation is known as John Wesley's rule. John Wesley was a minister who founded Methodism. (1703–1791)

6. I think that I shall never see a poem as lovely as a tree. **Joyce Kilmer (1886–1918) from *Trees and Other Poems*, George H. Duncan Co, 1914, p. 18.**

7. A teacher affects eternity. He can never tell where his influence stops. **Henry B. Adams (1838–1918), U.S. Historian, from the *Education of Henry Adams*, Chapter 20 (1907).**

8. Create in me a clean heart, O God; and renew a right spirit within me. **King David in Psalm 51:10.**

9. Go the the ant, thou sluggard; consider his ways, and be wise; **King Solomon in Proverbs 6:6.**

10. No man can serve two masters; for either he will hate the one, and love the other; or else he will hold to the one and despise the other. Ye cannot serve God and mammon. **Jesus in Matthew 6:24, from the Sermon on the Mount.**

11. Success is counted sweetest by those who ne'er succeed. **Emily Dickinson (1830–1886) from *The Complete Poems* (1955), #67, stanza 1.**

12. Genius is one percent inspiration and 99 percent perspiration. **Thomas Edison, (1847–1931).**

13. I have nothing to offer but blood, toil, tears, and sweat. **Sir Winston Churchill, May 13, 1940, in his first speech as Prime Minister to the House of Commons.**

14. To read well, that is, to read true books in a true spirit is a noble exercise. **Henry David Thoreau (1817–1862) from "Reading" in Walden (1854).**

15. I want to be alone. **Greta Garbo from the film, "Grand Hotel" in 1932.**

16. The universe is wider than our views of it. **Henry David Thoreau from the *Conclusion to Walden* (1854).**

17. Sin has many tools, but a lie is the handle which fits them all. **Oliver Wendall Holmes**

18. You must train children to their studies in a playful manner…. **Plato (427–347 BC) as recorded by Socrates in the *Republic*, Book 7, Sect. 537.**

19. Always do right—this will gratify some and astonish the rest. **Mark Twain, in a message to the Young People's Society in New York, Feb. 16, 1901.**

20. Let not him who is houseless pull down the house of another. **Abraham Lincoln, in a speech given March 21, 1864.**

21. If a man hasn't discovered something he will die for, he isn't fit to live. **Martin Luther King, Jr. (1929–1968).**

22. Our destiny is bound up with the destiny of every other American. **Bill Clinton, in a speech to his supporters in Little Rock Arkansas, November 4, 1992.**

23. Nothing you can do for children is ever wasted. **Garrison Keillor**

24. Kilroy was here. **WWII Graffiti that represented the world-wide presence of the United States.**

25. We will now discuss in a little more detail the Struggle for Existence. **Charles Darwin from the *Origin of the Species*, 1859.**

Read the following quotes. Find out who said them and why, and then separate them into categories according to what you feel is the main idea of each.

1. "Float like a butterfly, sting like a bee."

2. "We shall find peace. We shall hear the angels, we shall see the sky sparkling with diamonds."

3. "Winning isn't everything, it's the only thing."

4. "Mankind must put an end to war or war will put an end to mankind."

5. "I have a dream that one day on the red hills of Georgia the sons of former slaves and the sons of former slaveowners will be able to sit down together at the table of brotherhood."

6. "You can't live in a world all alone. Your brothers are here too."

7. "Winning isn't everything, but wanting to win is."

Winning:

1. "Float like a butterfly, sting like a bee." **Boxing creed devised by Drew Brown and adopted as Mohammed Ali's philosophy.**

3. "Winning isn't everything, it's the only thing." **Often attributed to football coach Red Sanders.**

7. "Winning isn't everything, but wanting to win is." **Vince Lombardi**

Peace:

4. "Mankind must put an end to war or war will put an end to mankind." **President Kennedy in a speech to the UN, 1961**

2. "We shall find peace. We shall hear the angels, we shall see the sky sparkling with diamonds." **Anton Chekov**

Brotherhood:

6. "You can't live in a world all alone. Your brothers are here too." **Albert Schweitzer on receiving the Nobel prize**

5. "I have a dream that one day on the red hills of Georgia the sons of former slaves and the sons of former slaveowners will be able to sit down together at the table of brotherhood." **MKL, Jr. in a civil rights speech in Washington, 1963**

Compare the following sets of quotations. Do you agree with the speaker or disagree? In your opinion, how are the quotes similar? How are they different? For each set, define your view and build a case to support your opinion.

I.

"I believe four ingredients are necessary for happiness: health, warm personal relations, sufficient means to keep you from want, and successful work." Bertrand Russell, 1964.

"There is only one happiness in life: to love and be loved." George Sand, 1962.

"What can be added to the happiness of a man who is in health, who is out of debt, and who has a clear conscience?" Adam Smith, 1759.

II.

"Life is a humbug." Thomas Carlyle

"Bah! Humbug!" Character of Ebenezer Scrooge in Charles Dickens' *A Christmas Carol*.

III.

"Life is a voyage." Victor Hugo in "The Toilers of the Sea."

"Life, Lucilius, is really a battle." Character of Seneca the Younger in "On Facing Hardships" by Richard Gummere, 1918.

"Life is one crisis after another." Richard Nixon, 1984.

IV.

"Life is a game—play to win." Al Newharth, 1993.

"Life is a game played on us while we are playing other games." Evan Esar, 1968.

V.

Ralph Waldo Emerson said, "Education is the drawing out of the soul."

Kahlil Gibran said, "In education the life of the mind proceeds to graduate from scientific experiments to intellectual theories, to spiritual reality, and then to God."

VI.

"Friendships multiply joys and divide griefs." Thomas Fuller, 1732.

"Friendship redoubleth joys and cutteth griefs in halves." Francis Bacon, 1625.

VII.

"'Tis great confidence in a friend to tll him your faults, greater to tell him His." Benjamin Franklin, 1751.

"It is one of the severest tests of friendship to tell your friend of his faults…to speak truth through loving words—that is friendship." Henry Ward Beecher, 1858.

VIII.

"Nothing discloses real character like the use of power." Robert G. Ingersoll, 1906.

"Character is power." Booker Washington, 1856–1915.

Quotable Quotes

Answers

Answers to these eight exercises will be quite subjective. Accept all justifiable answers. Look for evidence that the subject has voiced an opinion on the key topic of the set of quotes and has argued that opinion suitably. A strong argument will include evidence that the student has researched the speaker and the circumstances of the quotation as well as specific choices of words used. Arguments should be supported by examples.

Resources for Preparing Your Own InfoQuest Quotation Program:

Auguarde, Tony. (1991). *Oxford Dictionary of Modern Quotations*. Oxford University Press, New York.

Bartlett, John. (1992). *Bartlett's Familiar Quotations*.16th ed. Boston: Little, Brown and Company.

Oxford Dictionary of Quotations. (1996). NY: Oxford University Press.

Random House Webster's Quotationary. (1999). New York: Random House.

Reese, Nigel. (1995). *Brewer's Quotations and Phrase and Fable Dictionary*. Wellington House, Strand, London: Cassell Publishers.

Chapter *12*

Looking Into Literature

Children enjoy being read to from the time they can sit on someone's lap and listen to a familiar voice. From nursery rhymes to classic literature, the delight is always new. Even adults derive pleasure from a narrator reading or retelling a tale. The flow of the language, the emphasis on particular words, the repetition of sounds and more all create beauty and pleasure. The events that drive a character to behave as he does and what becomes of him keep us involved to the end of the tale.

> **"Literature is language charged with meaning."**
>
> *– Ezra Pound from ABC of Reading, Ch. 2 (as quoted in Bartlett's Quotations, 1992, p. 660).*

Students enjoy knowing more about their favorite authors, often reading all the books by a particular author or all the books in a series, or even reading only in a particular genre. Knowledge about authors, illustrators, series, and genre create interest and enthusiasm in lower grades and keep students reading while a knowledge of the classics of both American and world literature is considered a necessity for a good education in the upper grades.

Information Literacy Skills Related to Literary Research

Information literacy skills related to literary research include:

- Showing pleasure in visiting the media center

- Handling books, magazines, newspapers and other materials responsibly

- Knowing the procedure for borrowing and returning a book

- Identifying a favorite author, illustrator, character, story, and series

- Summarizing a favorite story

- Describing a favorite character

- Realizing the catalog provides information about title, author, publisher

- Identifying fiction and nonfiction authors

- Knowing call numbers for fiction and nonfiction

- Identifying title, author, and subject of a book

- Using the Dewey Decimal system to locate a book

- Alphabetizing by 1, 2, or 3 letters

- Retelling events in a story in own words

- Organizing events in a story in order

- Using graphic organizers to put events in a story in order

- Identifying classic American literature authors and titles

- Identifying classic World literature authors and titles

Questions and Answers on Literature

Great works of both American and world literature are the focus of this chapter. Subjects include notable children's literature, Caldecott and Newbery award winners, serials, trilogies, historical and science fiction, humorous and contemporary fiction, and famous short stories, plays, and novels from around the world. Resources for preparing your own *InfoQuest* literature program are listed at the end of this chapter.

Best Beginner Books

Preliminary

Questions

The following questions are designed to acquaint you with some of the best beginner books in children's literature. Look up the italicized keyword(s) and then answer the question.

1. In what year was the first *Dr. Seuss* book published?

2. What was the name of the first *Dr. Seuss* book published?

3. Who are the sisters of *Peter Rabbit*?

4. In which book do a tiger (Tigger), a donkey (Eeyore), a kangaroo (Roo), a bear, and a small boy enjoy adventures?

5. What is the title of a book about a little rebel named *Max*?

6. What type of character is *Corduroy*?

7. What is the motto of a little train that keeps trying to go up a hill?

8. What happened to the *Velveteen Rabbit*?

1. In what year was the first Dr. Seuss book published? **1957**

2. What was the name of the first Dr. Seuss book published? ***The Cat in the Hat* with just 175 words**

3. Who are the sisters of Peter Rabbit? **Flopsy, Mopsy, and Cottontail**

4. In which book do a tiger, a donkey, a kangaroo, a bear, and a small boy enjoy adventures? ***The Adventures of Winnie the Pooh***

5. What is the title of a book about a little rebel named Max? ***Where the Wild Things Are***

6. What type of character is Corduroy? **A bear**

7. What is the motto of a little train that keeps trying to go up a hill? **"I think I can, I think I can"**

8. What happened to the Velveteen Rabbit? **He became real**

The following questions are designed to acquaint you with some of the best early fiction in children's literature. Look up the bold type keyword(s) first and then answer the question.

1. Which Dr. Seuss book is about a boy who cannot remove his hat?

2. What is the title of a Caldecott award winner?

3. Who is the illustrator of *Space Case*?

4. Who is the main character in the *Magic School Bus* series?

5. What is the name of the popular historical fiction series for girls?

6. In *Ramona and Beezus*, what is Ramona's sister's name?

7. What is the title of a fiction book by James Howe?

8. In this book a little orphan girl is captured by a big friendly giant. What is the title?

9. Name the book in which two brothers raise unusual plants and keep losing their socks.

10. In which book do children pass through a magical wardrobe into an enchanted kingdom?

1. Which Dr. Seuss book is about a boy who cannot remove his hat? ***The 500 Hats of Bartholomew Cubbins***

2. What is the title of a Caldecott award winner? **Answers may vary**

3. Who is the illustrator of *Space Case?* **James Marshall**

4. Who is the main character in the *Magic School Bus* series? **Ms. Frizzle**

5. What is the name of the popular historical fiction series for girls? **American Girls or Dear America series**

6. In *Ramona and Beezus*, what is Ramona's sister's name? **Beatrice**

7. What is the title of a fiction book by James Howe? ***Bunnicula* (or other titles)**

8. In this book a little orphan girl is captured by a giant. **What is the title?** ***The BFG***

9. Name the book in which two brothers raise unusual plants and keep losing their socks. ***The Plant that Ate Dirty Socks***

10. In which book do children pass through a magical wardrobe into an enchanted kingdom? ***The Chronicles of Narnia* (any title)**

Literature Links

Intermediate

Questions

1. Which book tells how Amber Brown is feeling?

2. Who is the author of the *Anastasia* series?

3. Which author has written a trilogy—C.S. Lewis or J.R.R. Tolkein?

4. What is the name of a sequel to *Shiloh*?

5. What is the Roald Dahl book about a very large fruit?

6. Which book is about a school which is built the wrong way?

7. Who is the author of the *Redwall* series?

8. Name a title by Will Hobbs.

9. Who is the author of *A Wrinkle in Time?*

10. What is the title of a Newbery winner?

11. In which book does a young woman from Jamaica go to live with her New England relatives and befriend a Quaker woman accused of being a witch?

12. In which book does an old house which was once a station on the Underground Railroad help a family come to terms with their heritage?

1. Which book tells how Amber Brown is feeling? ***Amber Brown is Feeling Blue***

2. Who is the author of the *Anastasia* series? **Lois Lowry**

3. Which author has written a trilogy—C.S. Lewis or J.R.R. Tolkein? **J.R.R. Tolkein**

4. What is the name of a sequel to *Shiloh?* ***Shiloh Season***

5. What is the Roald Dahl book about a very large fruit? ***James and the Giant Peach***

6. Which book is about a school which is built the wrong way? ***Sideways Stories from Wayside School***

7. Who is the author of the *Redwall* series? **Brian Jacques**

8. Name a title by Will Hobbs. ***The Ghost Canoe* (or other title)**

9. Who is the author of *A Wrinkle in Time?* **Madeleine L'Engle**

10. What is the title of a Newbery winner? **(answers may vary)**

11. In which book does a young woman from Jamaica go to live with her New England relatives and befriend a Quaker woman accused of being a witch? ***The Witch of Blackbird Pond***

12. In which book does an old house which was once a station on the Underground Railroad help a family come to terms with their heritage? ***The House of Dies Drear***

1. Who was the author of *Moby Dick*? What else did he write? In your opinion, which of these works is the greatest and why?

2. Who was Ichabod Crane and what do you think made him a classic literary figure?

3. What characters in other great literary works are similar to Ebenezer Scrooge?

4. What do you think made Anne Frank's letters to Kitty so famous and so poignant?

5. How do you think French writer Alexander Dumas may have influenced his friend Jules Verne?

6. What do you think Romeo meant when he said, "Night's candles are burnt out and jocund days stands tiptoe on the misty mountain tops. I must be gone and live or stay and die."

7. What do you think the *Kon Tiki* proved?

8. In your opinion, what was the horror of "The Lottery"?

9. Why do you think Hester Prynne became a universal symbol of sin?

10. Explain what you think Holden Caufield represents?

11. For what do you think the two tramps in "Waiting for Godot' were waiting?

12. If you could name one children's author that you consider to be at the top of her craft, who would it be and why?

13. Among awards given for excellence in children's and young adult literature, there are the Newbery, the Coretta Scott King, the Christopher and others. Create your own award. Give it a title and explain the criteria for winning the award. Then select some titles that you feel are worthy of this award.

1. Who was the author of *Moby Dick*? What else did he write? In your opinion, which of these works is the greatest and why? **Herman Melville also wrote *Billy Budd*, *Benito Cereno*, and *Typee*, but *Moby Dick* has been the most enduring.**

2. Who was Ichabod Crane and what do you think made him a classic literary figure? **Ichabod Crane was legendary school teacher who becomes the victim of a frightening prank in "The Legend of Sleepy Hollow." He is a classic figure because all of us can identify and sympathize with this victim of a cruel, frightening prank.**

3. What characters in other great literary works are similar to Ebenezer Scrooge? **Dr. Seuss's the *Grinch* is another classic "scrooge."**

4. What do you think made Anne Frank's letters to Kitty so famous and so poignant? **Anne Frank's letters to Kitty are actually her diary which shows the coming of age of a young girl, her first love, and more during the horror of the Holocaust.**

5. How do you think French writer Alexander Dumas may have influenced his friend Jules Verne? **Dumas staged Verne's first play at his Parisian theater, which may have been just the enouragement Verne needed to give up law and write full-time.**

6. What do you think Romeo meant when he said, "Night's candles are burnt out and jocund days stands tiptoe on the misty mountain tops. I must be gone and live or stay and die." **Romeo meant that it would be disastrous, even deadly, for him to be found with Juliet after their romantic evening together.**

7. What do you think the *Kon Tiki* proved? ***Kon Tiki* proved that is was possible to travel across the ocean in a reed boat such as early civilizations might have built.**

8. In your opinion, what was the horror of "The Lottery"? **This Shirley Jackson short story's horror is that an entire town was willing to sacrifice an innocent person who drew a lottery number.**

9. Why do you think Hester Prynne became a universal symbol of sin? **Hester Prynne, the adulteress in *The Scarlett Letter* is a symbol of the shame and grief that sin can cause.**

10. Explain what you think Holden Caufield represents? **Holden Caufield represents the innocence of youth.**

11. For what do you think the two tramps in "Waiting for Godot' were waiting? **They were waiting for a change in circumstances, deliverance, purpose in life, perhaps God.**

12. If you could name one children's author that you consider to be at the top of his craft, who would it be and why? **Answers may vary. Accept all supported answers.**

13. Among awards given for excellence in children's and young adult literature, there are the Newbery, the Coretta Scott King, the Christopher and others. Create your own award. Give it a title and explain the criteria for winning the award. Then select some titles that you feel are worthy of this award. **Answers may vary.**

Resources for Preparing Your Own InfoQuest Literature Program:

Arbuthnot, May Hill et al. (1971). *The Arbuthnot Anthology of Children's Literature*. Glenview, Ill.: Scott, Foresman and Co.

Benet's Readers Encyclopedia 4th ed. (1996). NY: Harper Collins Publishers.

Best of the Best for Children. (1992). NY: Random House.

Binghame, Jane and Graycie Scholt. (1980). *Fifteen Centuries of Children's Literature*. Westport, Ct: Greenwood Press.

Gillespie, John T. and Corinne J. Naden. (1990). *Best Books for Children*. NY: R.R. Bowker.

Harvey, Sir Paul. (1986). *The Oxford Companion to Classical Literature*. NY: Oxford University Press.

Holman, C. Hugh and William Harmon. (1986). *Handbook to Literature*. NY: Macmillan.

Oxford Companion to Classical Literature. (1989). NY: Oxford University Press.

Chapter 13

Grazing Through Geography

One of the most intriguing fields of study is geography. From the time we can observe this world around us, the physical features that define our neighborhoods, home towns, have a profound effect on our lifestyles, habits, cultures, and even our senses. When we begin to venture out past the familiar territory of our immediate surroundings, our horizons broaden from the sense of how foreign cultures are influenced by their environments.

The political divisions of the world are equally intriguing as we come to understand that the world's inhabited continents are all divided into nations large and small, which are in turn divided into cities and townships.

Geography is the study of political divisions and physical features that make up this wonderful planet we call home. A study of geography include latitude and longitude, time zones, regions, mountains, rivers, oceans, lakes, cities, states, nations, continents, and more.

> **"Journey all over the universe in a map, without the expense and fatigue of traveling, without suffering the inconveniences of heat, cold, hunger, and thirst."**
>
> *– Miguel de Cervantes (Don Quixote, 1615, book III, Ch. 6, p. 479)*

Information Literacy Skills Associated with Geographical Research

Information literacy skills associated with geographical research include:

- Realizing that the school library media center, the school library media specialist, other individuals, books, magazines, newspapers, computer databases, software, and the Internet are sources of information or assistance with information

- Showing pleasure in visiting the school library media center in supervised and unsupervised groups or individually

- Visits the school library media center frequently for both pleasure and research purposes

- Visits the school library media center for sources other than just electronic media

- Feels comfortable in the library media center working independently or with a group

- Uses time purposefully in the library media center without supervision

- Demonstrates responsibility in the use of library media center materials

- Knows how to correctly handle books, magazines, newspapers, computer hardware, software, and peripherals

- Knows correct procedure for borrowing or returning a book, placing a book on hold or reserve, searching the catalog, searching other library catalogs, ordering materials through interlibrary loan

- Can communicate what he wants to know

- Recognizes that the catalog provides information about title, author, publishers, illustrator, copyright date, summary of contents, related subjects, bibliographical information

- Realizes that sources can be both print and nonprint

- Realizes that print and nonprint resources can serve different functions

- Realizes that the same source may vary in print and nonprint formats

- Sources of information can be primary or secondary

- The best sources of information fit specific criteria

- Feels comfortable seeking or giving assistance

- Can accurately formulate a question or theory

- Can restate question in own words

- Can formulate a list of related topics

- Can broaden or narrow topic

- Can relate what is known to what is unknown

- Can brainstorm for a list of possible sources of information

- Can identify the location of periodicals, nonfiction, reference, audiovisual and software materials

- Can identify subject headings and subheadings

- Can skim or scan for information

- Can read captions, use contents, index

- Give main idea of stories or subject of articles

- Can use almanac to locate a statistic, atlas to locate a map, compass rose for orientation

- Can interpret a map key

- Can determine distance using a map scale

- Can interpret information from a chart or graph

- Can paraphrase information

- Can accurately cite and paraphrase information

- Can proofread for spelling, punctuation and grammatical errors, omissions, insertions, indentions, tense and other errors

- Can utilize word processing, spreadsheet, and database programs to organize information

- Can log on to the Internet and use a browser

- Can perform an electronic search using keywords, Boolean strategies, truncation, parentheses

- Compares information from various sources

- Writes notes on main ideas

- Can outline and use notes to write paragraphs in own words

- Can use a computer to organize files into folders, back up files, find files, get help

- Can create multimedia presentation

- Can create, upload, and maintain a web page

- Compares and contrasts information to determine contradictions, validity, bias

Questions and Answers on Geographical Research

This chapter focuses on latitude and longitude, capital cities, distinguishing characteristics of some of the various part of the world and a world travel game. Questions are offered on all four levels and include a wide variety of skills. Resources for planning your own *InfoQuest* geography program are listed at the end of this chapter.

An Attitude About Latitude

Preliminary

Questions

1. Which U.S. city is closest to the equator: Jacksonville, Florida or San Diego, California?

2. Which city is closest to the North Pole: Vancouver, BC or Montreal, Quebec?

3. Which state extends farther north: Michigan or Minnesota?

4. Which city extends farther south: Corpus Christi, TX or Orlando, Florida?

5. What point is the U.S. is the farthest east: Massachusetts or Maine?

6. Which point is closest to another continent: Florida to South America, Alaska to Russia, or Hawaii to Asia?

7. Which location is farther north: Queen Elizabeth Island or the Aleutian Islands?

8. The International Date Line separates what two continents?

9. Which of the Great Lakes extends farthest north?

10. Which U.S. city is farthest from the equator: Milwaukee, WI, Detroit, MI, or Rochester, NY?

1. Which U.S. city is closest to the equate: Jacksonville, Florida or San Diego, California? **Jacksonville, Florida**

2. Which city is closest to the North Pole: Vancouver, BC or Montreal, Quebec? **Vancouver, BC**

3. Which state extends farther north: Michigan or Minnesota? **Minnesota**

4. Which city extends farther south: Corpus Christi, TX or Orlando, Florida? **Corpus Christi, TX**

5. What point in the U.S. is the farthest east: Massachusetts or Maine? **Maine**

6. Which point is closest to another continent: Florida to South America, Alaska to Russia, or Hawaii to Asia? **Alaska to Russia**

7. Which location is farther north: Queen Elizabeth Island or the Aleutian Islands? **Queen Elizabeth Island**

8. The International Date Line separates what two continents? **North America and Asia**

9. Which of the Great Lakes extends farthest north: Michigan or Ontario? **Ontario**

10. Which U.S. city is farthest from the equator: Milwaukee, WI, Detroit, MI, or Rochester, NY? **Rochester, NY**

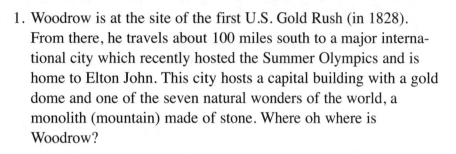
1. Woodrow is at the site of the first U.S. Gold Rush (in 1828). From there, he travels about 100 miles south to a major international city which recently hosted the Summer Olympics and is home to Elton John. This city hosts a capital building with a gold dome and one of the seven natural wonders of the world, a monolith (mountain) made of stone. Where oh where is Woodrow?

2. Woodrow has a few Rupees to spend in a city also known as Mumbai which has grown so quickly that there are insufficient jobs and homes for its people. As a result, there are large areas of waterfront slums. Woodrow is amazed to see cows wandering in the streets and people pulling rickshaws. Where oh where is Woodrow?

3. Woodrow has become interested in volcanoes and decides he wants to see the world's tallest volcano. According to his almanac, this volcano, CERRO ACONCAGUA, is 22,830 ft. high, and could produce some powerful eruptions in this country. He isn't too worried, though, because this volcano is not inactive. Where oh where is Woodrow?

4. Woodrow is visiting Kilimanjaro, the highest mountain in this nation, which is also home to beautiful Lake Victoria. Woodrow is interested in seeing the Serengeti Plains Animal Park before he departs. Where oh where is Woodrow?

5. Woodrow is visiting Citlaltepetl, the highest mountain in this country, which stands 19,551 feet high. He also plans to visit the resort city of Oaxaca, to the west, and perhaps look for pyramids on the eastern peninsula. Where oh where is Woodrow?

6. Woodrow is landing in Kimpo International Airport, one of the world's busiest. He is visiting a city which once hosted the Olympics. For lunch, Woodrow tasted kimchi, a national staple, and found it very tasty. Where oh where is Woodrow?

7. Woodrow has become a coffee drinker. He is visiting the right country now, because this country is the world's #1 COFFEE PRODUCER. He also wants to see the huge river full of carnivorous fish in the northern half of this nation and perhaps spot a sloth. Where oh where is Woodrow?

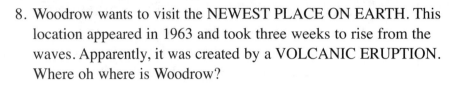

8. Woodrow wants to visit the NEWEST PLACE ON EARTH. This location appeared in 1963 and took three weeks to rise from the waves. Apparently, it was created by a VOLCANIC ERUPTION. Where oh where is Woodrow?

9. Woodrow has heard a lot about the WORLD'S LARGEST WATERFALL. According to his references, this waterfall is 3,212 ft. high and plunges down the side of a cliff. Woodrow thinks its name, ANGEL FALLS, is appropriate, as he is awed by the sight. Where oh where is Woodrow?

10. Woodrow is visiting in a country with THE LARGEST FOREST IN THE WORLD. It covers a total area of 3.5 million square miles. This country is one of the TOP PRODUCERS of hardwoods. It also has the largest lake in the world and a huge iceberg, NOVAYA ZEMLYA, 260 miles long. Where oh where is Woodrow?

11. Woodrow is in a location which is on of the WORLD'S LARGEST PENINSULAS, some 580,000 square miles long. This location contains the beautiful ALEUTIAN ISLANDS, and is home to a multitude of wildlife. Where oh where is Woodrow?

12. Woodrow has decided to visit GREAT BEAR LAKE, one of the largest lakes in the world. It is located in the same country as the BAY OF FUNDY, where there is the greatest difference in low and high tides, some 52 feet. Where oh where is Woodrow?

1. Woodrow is at the site of the first U.S. Gold Rush (in 1828). From there, he travels about 100 miles south to a major international city which recently hosted the Summer Olympics and is home to Elton John. This city hosts a capital building with a gold dome and one of the seven natural wonders of the world, a mountain made of stone. Where oh where is Woodrow? **Atlanta, Georgia, USA**

2. Woodrow has a few Rupees to spend in a city also known as Mumbai which has grown so quickly that there are insufficient jobs and homes for its people. As a result, there are large areas of waterfront slums. Woodrow is amazed to see cows wandering in the streets and people pulling rickshaws. Where oh where is Woodrow? **Bombay, India**

3. Woodrow has become interested in volcanoes and decides he wants to see the world's tallest volcano. According to his almanac, this volcano, CERRO ACONCAGUA, is 22,830 ft. high, and could produce some powerful eruptions in this country. He isn't too worried, though, because this volcano is not inactive. Where oh where is Woodrow? **Andes Mts. in Argentina**

4. Woodrow is visiting Kilimanjaro, the highest mountain in this nation, which is also home to beautiful Lake Victoria. Woodrow is interested in seeing the Serengeti Plains Animal Park before he departs. Where oh where is Woodrow? **Tanzania**

5. Woodrow is visiting Citlaltepetl, the highest mountain in this country, which stands 19,551 feet high. He also plans to visit the resort city of Oaxaca, to the west, and perhaps look for pyramids on the eastern peninsula. Where oh where is Woodrow? **Mexico**

6. Woodrow is landing in Kimpo International Airport, one of the world's busiest. He is visiting a city which once hosted the Olympics. For lunch, Woodrow tasted kimchi, a national staple, and found it very tasty. Where oh where is Woodrow? **Seoul, Korea**

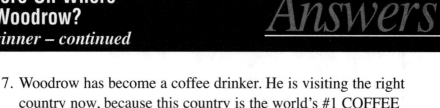
7. Woodrow has become a coffee drinker. He is visiting the right country now, because this country is the world's #1 COFFEE PRODUCER. He also wants to see the huge river full of carnivorous fish in the northern half of this nation and perhaps spot a sloth. Where oh where is Woodrow? **Amazon River in Brazil**

8. Woodrow wants to visit the NEWEST PLACE ON EARTH. This island appeared in 1963 and took three weeks to rise from the waves, similar to Hawaii, but unlike Hawaii, it is neither tropical or in the same ocean. Apparently, it was created by a VOLCANIC ERUPTION. Where oh where is Woodrow? **The island of Surtsey**

9. Woodrow has heard a lot about the WORLD'S LARGEST WATERFALL. According to his references, this waterfall is 3,212 ft. high and plunges down the side of a cliff. Woodrow thinks its name, ANGEL FALLS, is appropriate, as he is awed by the sight. Where oh where is Woodrow? **Venezuela**

10. Woodrow is visiting in a country with THE LARGEST FOREST IN THE WORLD. It covers a total area of 3.5 million square miles. This country is one of the TOP PRODUCERS of hardwoods. It also has the largest lake in the world and a huge iceberg, NOVAYA ZEMLYA, 260 miles long. Where oh where is Woodrow? **Russia**

11. Woodrow is in a location which is on of the WORLD'S LARGEST PENINSULAS, some 580,000 square miles long. This location contains the beautiful ALEUTIAN ISLANDS, and is home to a multitude of wildlife. Where oh where is Woodrow? **Alaska, USA**

12. Woodrow has decided to visit GREAT BEAR LAKE, one of the largest lakes in the world. It is located in the same country as the BAY OF FUNDY, where there is the greatest difference in low and high tides, some 52 feet. Where oh where is Woodrow? **Canada**

1. Compare and contrast Taiwan and Thailand.

2. What is the difference in an iceblink and an iceberg?

3. Compare and contrast the Rocky Mountains to the Appalachian Mountains.

4. What is the difference between a marsh and a bayou?

5. How do Florida beaches compare to Hawaiian beaches?

6. Compare the world's tallest building to the world's tallest mountain.

1. Compare and contrast Taiwan and Thailand. **Both had former names: Taiwan was once Formosa, and Thailand was once Siam. Both are growing Asian nations. Taiwan is much smaller than Thailand; it is an island that lies in the Pacific Ocean and is surrounded on all sides by water. Thailand is a large mainland nation and is surrounded by Cambodia, Laos, Myanmar, Vietnam and Malaysia. It has the Gulf of Thailand on one side. Both Taiwan and Thailand raise rice as a major crop, but Taiwan's economy is booming from the electronics trade.**

2. What is the difference in an iceblink and an iceberg? **An iceblink is a coastal ice cliff while an iceberg floats in water.**

3. Compare and contrast the Rocky Mountains to the Appalachian Mountains. **The Rocky Mountains are much higher than the Appalachian Mountains and have a longer range, extending far into Canada. The Appalachian Mountains are older than the Rockies and the peaks are more rounded and worn. The Rockies are in the Western half of North American and the Appalachians are in the east.**

4. What is the difference between a marsh and a bayou? **A bayou is a slow-moving stream that is a part of a larger body of water such as a large creek or river. A bayou is composed of water, as opposed to a marsh which is soggy, water-soaked land, usually low-lying and close to a body of water.**

5. How do Florida beaches compare to Hawaiian beaches? **Hawaii is composed predominantly of volcanic rock and its beaches have black sand formed from lava. The Hawaiian islands are similar in flora and fauna and have a similar temperature to the South Florida beaches, but Hawaiian beaches are on the Pacific Ocean and Florida beaches can be on the Atlantic Ocean, the Gulf of Mexico, or the Caribbean.**

6. Compare the world's tallest building to the world's tallest mountain. **Mt. Everest, the world's tallest mountain, is twenty times taller than the Sears Tower.**

1. A seismograph is a modern instrument used to measure earthquakes. The first seismograph was invented by the Chinese and consisted of a pot that caught metal balls which fell off the mouths of dragons' statues when an earthquake was imminent. Do you think a modern seismograph is better than the ancient Chinese version? Can you create a means of predicting earthquakes? Explain how it works.

2. Recommend a way to make buildings safer from natural disasters such as floods, tornadoes, hurricanes, earthquakes. What kind of building would you design and why?

3. Devise a way to make more of the earth's continents habitable for our growing population. Which are would you select— deserts, mountains, or polar regions? Why?

4. Study the tectonic plates theory and Pangaea. If the continents did indeed break off and move away from each other, they are still moving apart. Design a map to show what you think the continents may look like 50 million years from now. Support your answer with facts and details.

5. Why do you think an area in the Pacific Ocean is called the "Pacific Ring of Fire?" What are some things that result from this phenomenon? Do you think it will ever change? Predict what may happen in this area in the next 50 years.

6. Some of the largest mountains in the world were formed when two of the Earth's plates collided with each other, pushing up the rock to form mountains. This growth occurred over billions of years. Do you think these mountains are still growing? Determine what effect you think this growth might have on the Earth one million years from now.

7. Off the coast of Florida there is an underwater hotel. Its guests must put on scuba diving equipment and dive to its entrance. Do you think this is a concept that will become popular—to build living space in the ocean? Argue both sides of the issue.

8. Consider the effects that industrialization has had on the environment: water, air and soil pollution, global warming, deforestation. If you could pick one of the problems and undo the damage, what would it be and why? How would you solve the problem. Explain your answer.

1. The Chinese seismograph was a 4 headed statue which had balls which dropped from dragons' mouths into frogs' mouths. The sides of the statue on which the balls fell indicated the epicenter of the earthquake. The modern seismograph consists of a pen that is attached to a tubular roll of paper. When the device is jarred by an earthquake, the pen records the quivering of the earth in jagged marks on the paper. The depth of the marks indicates the degree of rocking of the earth and the strength of the quake. Answers may vary on students' own devices and their opinions of the modern vs. the Chinese seismographs.

2. People have devised many means of securing homes from natural disasters. Homes in flood-prone areas have been built on stilts, or walls of sandbags surround the property near coasts or riverbanks where flooding from strong tides or rising rivers is common. Seawalls are built to prevent flooding of oceanfront property during hurricanes. Buildings have been built with steel framework to strengthen them from earthquake damage. Plexiglass and shatterproof glass has been used to prevent tornado damage. Answers may vary on students' own designs.

3. Cave drawings indicate that desert regions in Africa were once lush with vegetation. Cities such as LasVegas and SanDiego have been built on desert lands. Perhaps with the proper irrigation, more desert cities could be built. Mountainous dwellings are common but mainly for ski enthusiasts. However, mountain homes in lower mountainous regions are a possibility. With proper materials and insulation, polar regions can be habitated but food and water supplies are critical. Answers may vary on students' selections and designs.

4. Student renderings may include a division of North and South America, a change in coastal areas indicating that cities such as San Francisco and others are no longer, perhaps some new island regions similar to Surtsey, and a change in the Mediterranean region. Answers may vary.

5. The ring of fire is a circle of underwater volcanoes in the Pacific Ocean. Eruptions from these may cause islands to form, tsunamis to damage the coastlines and more. Answers may vary.

6. Scientists have indicated that the Himalayas are still growing. As mountains rise, danger from avalanches, runoff from mountain streams, new caves and caverns may form. Answers may vary.

7. Answers may vary but should indicate research has been done to substantiate an argument for either side.

8. Answers may vary.

Resources for Preparing Your Own InfoQuest Geography Program:

Burnham, Robert. (2000). *Reader's Digest Children's Atlas of the Universe*. Pleasantville, NY: Reader's Digest.

Butterfield, Moira. (1992). *1000 Facts About the Earth*. NY: Kingfisher Books.

National Geographic U.S. Atlas for Young Explorers. (1999). Washington, D.C.: National Geographic Society.

Rand McNally Children's World Atlas. (1992). Chicago: Rand McNally.

Williams, Brian. (1992). *Kingfisher Reference Atlas*. NY: Kingfisher Books.

Chapter 14

Honing in on History

Throughout recorded history, various civilizations have been fascinating, particularly the inventive Greeks, the industrious Egyptians, the mysterious Celts, the barbarous Vikings. It is inspiring to investigate how civilizations lived and died, educated their young, governed themselves, dressed, ate, made tools, and expressed themselves. Seeing how others before us lived and died ultimately helps us to gain a better understanding of ourselves. The study of the events in civilizations before ours is history.

> "…as a matter of fact, man himself is his most important creation and achievement of the continuous human effort, the record of what we call history."
>
> *– Erich Fromm (from Escape from Freedom, 1941, Chapter 1).*

Information Literacy Skills Associated with Historical Research

Information literacy skills associated with historic research include:

- Realizing that the media center, the media specialist, books, magazines, newspapers, computer databases, and the Internet are a source of information or assistance with information

- Showing pleasure in visiting the library media center in supervised or unsupervised groups, or individually

- Demonstrating responsible use of library media center materials

- Knowing how to correctly handle books, magazines, newspapers, computers and software, audio visual equipment

- Knowing the correct procedure for borrowing and returning a resource, placing a resource on hold or reserve, searching other media center collections, requesting a resource through interlibrary loan

- Communicating what she wants to know

- Visiting the library media center frequently for pleasure and research purposes

- Feels comfortable in the library media center either working independently or in a group

- Feels comfortable with the media center staff and feels comfortable either asking for or giving assistance

- Recognizing that the catalog provides information about title, author, illustrator, publisher, subject, related subjects, summary of contents, bibliographical information

- Realizing that resources can be both print and nonprint

- Realizing that print and nonprint resources serve different functions

- Realizing that the same resource may vary in print and nonprint formats

- Realizing that the best resources fit specific criteria

- Accurately formulating a question

- Restating a question in own words

- Brainstorming for related topics and possible resources

- Knowing location of different types of resources in media center

- Locating a subject in an encyclopedia

- Using a table of contents and index

- Skimming and scanning for information

- Using headings, subheadings, titles, subtitles, captions, and more to locate information

- Logging on to the Internet

- Using a browser and search engine

- Performing a search using keywords, truncation, parentheses, phraseology, Boolean search strategies

- Using see and see also references

- Broadening or narrowing a topic

Historical research lends itself well to a variety of presentation formats, especially multimedia. Some creative students may particularly enjoy creating a slide show with audio clips or a videotape to present their work. Some of the specific organization and presentation skills related to research on history include:

- Proofreading for spelling, punctuation, or grammatical errors

- Summarizing information found

- Writing notes

- Paraphrasing and citing references accurately and correctly compiling bibliographical information

- Identifies irrelevant statements

- Utilizes graphic organizers for search results

- Utilizes outlines, draw and paint programs, or multimedia programs for presenting search results

- Utilizing word processing, spreadsheet, or database programs to organize information

- Utilizing charts, graphs, tables, and pictures to illustrate points

- Retelling information in own words

- Preparing a newscast, a speech, or narrating a documentary video or audiotape

- Writing information learned in own words in an editorial, newsletter, report

- Writing appropriate topic sentences

- Communicating information in complete sentences

- Organizing information into paragraphs

- Creating appropriate titles for work

- Composing an introduction and conclusion

- Supporting all points made with effective, authoritative statistics

- Fitting presentation to audience

- Integrating appropriate media into presentation

Questions and Answers on History

This chapter focuses on the imaginative inventors, the deadly disasters, the historic happenings that changed our lives, and the legends that have fascinated us for centuries. Resources for preparing your own *InfoQuest* history research are listed at the end of this chapter.

Imaginative Inventors

Preliminary

1. Who invented the ball-point pen?

2. Who is known as the inventor of the telescope?

3. Whose name is synonymous with bubblegum and is also its inventor?

4. To whom is the invention of the hula hoop credited?

5. Credit is given to which man for the invention of the television?

6. Where and when was paper first used?

7. Who is known for inventing the printing press?

8. This man invented the steam boat. Who was he?

9. What team invented the microchip?

10. What famous inventor created the submarine?

11. Where did Velcro originate?

12. Whose name is known for creating the first automobile with an internal combustion engine?

13. In addition to many other inventions, this man created the first motion picture camera. Who was he?

1. Who invented the ball-point pen? **Ladislao Biro, a Hungarian artist**

2. Who is known as the inventor of the telescope? **Galileo**

3. Whose name is synonymous with bubblegum and is also its inventor? **Fleer**

4. To whom is the invention of the hula hoop credited? **Richard Knerr and Authur Melin invented the hula hoop in 1958.**

5. Credit is given to which man for the invention of the television? **Philo Taylor Farnsworth**

6. Where and when was paper first used? **China in A.D. 105**

7. Who is known for inventing the printing press? **Gutenberg**

8. This man invented to steam boat. Who was he? **Robert Fulton**

9. What team invented the microchip? **Jack St. Clair Kilby and Robert Norton Noyce**

10. What famous inventor created the submarine? **Leonardo da Vinci**

11. Where did Velcro originate? **Velcro was invented by a Swiss engineer, Georges de Mistral**

12. Whose name is known for creating the first automobile with an internal combustion engine? **Carl Benz**

13. In addition to many other inventions, this man created the first motion picture camera. Who was he? **Thomas Edison**

Deadly Disasters

Preliminary

Questions

1. The San Francisco earthquake of 1906 was called the "worst natural disaster in U.S. history. " How many people died in the fire?

2. What was discovered about the safety devices on board ship after the *Titanic* struck an iceberg in 1912?

3. What mode of transportation ended when the Hindenburg burst into flames in1937?

4. One legend about the Chicago fire of 1871 that says that a cow kicked over a lantern, but in fact the fire began in what way?

5. The freak volcanic eruption that occurred in Pompeii resulted in what?

6. Historians discovered that the Black Plague was spread by what means?

7. When Mt. St. Helens erupted in Washington state in 1980 what happened to the area besides a blanket of volcanic ash?

8. What was the Chernobyl accident in Ukraine known as?

1. The San Francisco earthquake of 1906 was called the "worst natural disaster in U.S. history. " How many people died in the fire? **452**

2. What was the discovered about the safety devices on board ship after the Titanic struck an iceberg in 1912? **1,500 people died due to insufficient life boats**

3. What mode of transportation ended when the Hindenburg burst into flames in 1937? **It was the end of dirigible transportation**

4. One legend about the Chicago fire of 1871 that says that a cow kicked over a lantern, but in fact the fire began in what way? **A legend says that a cow kicked over a lantern, but in fact the fire began in a barn on the west side.**

5. The freak volcanic eruption that occurred in Pompeii resulted in what? **The city was completely buried in volcanic ash.**

6. Historians discovered that the Black Plague was spread by what means? **Fleas that bit rats carrying the plague spread it to people**

7. When Mt. St. Helens erupted in Washington state in 1980 what happened to the area besides a blanket of volcanic ash? **Fires, mudslides, floods**

8. What was the Chernobyl accident in Ukraine known as? **The worst nuclear reaction in history**

1. Compare the Wright Brothers historic flight to Lindbergh's.

2. Compare and contrast the controversy over Peary's trip to the North Pole and Cook's.

3. King Tut's tomb was discovered in 1939. Do you think this event had a greater impact than the discovery of the Dead Sea Scrolls? Explain your answer.

4. Compare the discovery of penicillin to the discovery of smallpox vaccine.

5. In your opinion, was Black Tuesday or the Black Plague a greater disaster?

6. Compare the bombing of Pearl Harbor to the bombing of Hiroshima.

7. How do you feel test tube baby Louise Brown compares to the cloned sheep Dolly?

8. In your opinion, was walking on the moon or manning a space station a greater accomplishment?

1. Compare the Wright Brothers' historic flight to Lindbergh's. **While the Wright Brothers' flight was short, Lindbergh's flight lasted 33 hours. The danger of flying over sea was much greater than the danger of flying over land. But, the Wright Brothers' historic first flight enabled Lindbergh to later fly across the ocean. Lindbergh would not have been able to make his historic flight had it not been for the Wright Brothers' making theirs. Students' answers may vary, but should indicate research and thought on the question.**

2. Compare and contrast the controversy over Peary's trip to the North Pole and Cook's. **It was most controversial as to which explorer arrived first at the North Pole but today Peary is generally credited by Congress and the scientific community with the first arrival, even though Cook claimed to have accomplished the first nearly a year earlier.**

3. King Tut's tomb was discovered in 1939. Do you think this event had a greater impact than the discovery of the Dead Sea Scrolls? Explain your answer. **Answers may vary but should be well supported.**

4. Compare the discovery of penicillin to the discovery of smallpox vaccine. **Student opinions and answers may vary. Accept all supported answers.**

5. In your opinion, was Black Tuesday or the Black Plague a greater disaster? **Black Tuesday was a financial disaster while the Black Plague was a life-threatening disaster. Student answers may vary but should but well supported.**

6. Compare the bombing of Pearl Harbor to the bombing of Hiroshima. **The surprise Japanese attack on Pearl Harbor in 1941 was devastating. About 3,000 Americans lost their lives and 19 battleships were either sunk or damaged. Twenty-eight Japanese planes and three submarines were lost. A result of the attack was that the U.S. declared war on Japan. The bombing of Hiroshima in 1945 forced Japan to surrender to the US and ended the second world war. A result of this bombing was that the idea of warfare was forever changed. The United Nations was formed to ensure world peace. Student answers may vary on this question, but should reflect research and thought. Accept all supported answers.**

7. How do you feel test tube baby Louise Brown compares to the cloned sheep Dolly? **Answers may vary, but cloning is still a very controversial issue while test-tube babies have gained acceptance as a means of conquering infertility.**

8. In your opinion, was walking on the moon or manning a space station a greater accomplishment? **We have successfully accomplished several moon landings and repeated space walks. In 1993 we cooperated with Russia to joint venture a manned space station. Student opinions may vary on which was the greater accomplishment. Accept all supported answers.**

Fact or Legend?

Advanced

Carefully consider reports of the following. Based on the stories that have been handed down from generation to generation, do you believe these figures or places were historical or legendary? For each one, explain what you believe and justify your answer.

1. Atlantis

2. Davy Crockett

3. King Arthur

4. Johnny Appleseed

5. Daniel Boone

6. Robin Hood

7. Gilgamesh

8. Odysseus

Carefully consider reports of the following. Based on the stories that have been handed down from generation to generation, do you believe these figures or places were historical or legendary? For each one, explain what you believe and justify your answer.

Answers may vary, as they are based on personal beliefs as well as research to support an opinion. Of the legendary heroes on the list, Davy Crockett, Daniel Boone and Johnny Appleseed were known to exist but tales about them have been greatly exaggerated. Accept all justified answers.

Resources for Preparing Your Own InfoQuest History Program:

Clements, John. (1975). *Chronology of the U.S.* New York: McGraw-Hill.

Colonial America. (1998). Danbury, CT: Grolier Education.

Kingfisher History Encyclopedia. (1999). New York: Larousse Kingfisher Chambers.

Moss, Joyce and George Wilson. (1996). *Profiles in World History—Significant Events and the People Who Shaped Them.* New York: Gale Research.

Chapter 15

Boning Up on Biography

People and their accomplishments, both good and bad, are always interesting. Note the popularity of *People* magazine, the tabloids, and television programming such as Entertainment Tonight and the E! Channel.

Of the millions of people who were born, lived, and died upon this Earth, a few have stood out for their wit, humor, achievements, leadership, inventions, discoveries, and more. These individuals, through a strong commitment to their calling, have changed the world. Their example is worth knowing about, and often, emulating. They inspire, motivate, challenge and invite curiosity. These individuals are the subjects of biographies.

> **"Biographies are but the clothes and buttons of the man."**
>
> *– Samuel Clemens (Autobiography, 1924, vol. 1 as quoted in Bartlett's Quotations, 1992, p. 528).*

Information Literacy Skills Associated with Biographical Research

The information literacy skills associated with biographical research include:

- Realizing that the school library media center, the school library media specialist, books, magazines, newspapers, computer databases, and the Internet are a source of information or assistance with information

- Showing pleasure in visiting the school library media center in supervised or unsupervised groups, or individually

- Using time purposefully in the media center

- Demonstrating responsibility in use of library media center materials

- Knowing how to correctly handle books, magazines, newspapers, computers, software, peripherals, and audiovisual equipment

- Knowing correct procedure for borrowing and returning a book, placing an item on hold or reserve, searching the catalog, searching another library catalog, searching the Internet, and ordering materials through interlibrary loans

- Realizing that the catalog provides information about author, title, illustrator, publisher, subject, related subjects, summary of content, and bibliographical information

- Realizing that sources can be print or nonprint

- Realizing that print and nonprint sources serve different functions

- Realizing that the same source can vary in print and nonprint formats

- Realizing that sources can be primary or secondary

- Realizing that criteria can help in selection of appropriate resources

- Feeling comfortable working independently or in a group

- Feeling comfortable asking for or giving assistance

- Communicating what he wants to know

- Formulating a question or theory to research

- Broadening or narrowing a question

- Brainstorming a list or related topics

- Knowing location or non-fiction, periodical, reference, audiovisual, and computer software resources

- Locating a subject in an encyclopedia

- Locating different types of resources with assistance

- Interpreting information from a chart, graph, table or picture

- Paraphrasing information located in a resource

- Proofreading for spelling, punctuation, and grammatical errors

- Using computer to open, save, delete, move, rename files and print documents

- Using word processing, spreadsheet, database, and multimedia software to organize information gathered

- Logging on to the Internet and using a browser

- Performing an electronic search using keywords, truncation, Boolean strategies

Biographical research is interesting to present in creative formats from assuming the role of an individual and acting it out to dramatically presenting events in that individual's life on a newscast, to editorializing significant events to creating a multimedia presentation. Students often enjoy role-playing opportunities or creating their own videotaped documentaries. Information literacy skills associated with organizing and presenting biographical information include:

- Writing notes

- Organizing notes into an outline

- Proofreading for omissions, insertions, indentions, tense and other errors

- Using electronic proofreading tools

- Using a variety of reference tools and knows the purpose of each

- Using individual biographies and collective biographies to research

- Selecting appropriate content related to search criteria to support topic

- Selecting appropriate format for presentation

- Putting events in order

- Summarizing important details

- Writes appropriate topic sentence

- Writing introduction and conclusion

- Utilizing graphic organizers for search results

- Recognizing bias, contradictions,

- Distinguishing between fact and opinion

- Identifying different types of writing such as narrative, persuasive, and recognizing purpose for each

- Judging currency, authority, validity of a resource prior to use

- Compiling bibliographical informaton

- Correctly paraphrasing, quoting, and citing references

- Preparing speech, narrative, newscast or other oral presentation of information

- Preparing editorial, newsletter, report, or other written presentation of information

- Visually displaying information in a poster, videotape, chart, graph, slide show

- Communicating in complete sentences

- Writing appropriate headings, titles

- Editing

Questions and Answers on Biographies

The individuals whose lives are the focus of this chapter are both American and international, politicians, scientists, activists, athletes, entertainers, inventors, military leaders, philosophers, and notorious notables. The following questions on all four levels include powerful people, famous figures, notorious notables, and a challenging "who dunnit" exercise.

Resources for planning your own *InfoQuest* biography program are listed at the end of this chapter.

The following questions are designed to help you become familiar with powerful people. Look up the italicized keyword(s) first and then answer the question.

1. What does the "D" in *Dwight D. Eisenhower* stand for?

2. Who became known as the *man without a country*?

3. Who is the record holder for the *most patents* given to an individual?

4. For what was *Marie Curie* awarded a Nobel Prize?

5. After *Rosa Parks* refused to give up her seat on the bus, who organized a bus boycott?

6. Who was the *first woman pictured on a U.S. Postage stamp*?

7. What does the "S" in *Harry S. Truman* stand for?

8. Who is *Cassius Clay*?

9. *Who was responsible for the voice of the early Mickey Mouse?*

10. *Louis Armstrong* invented a singing technique known as scat. What is it?

1. What does the "D" in Dwight D. Eisenhower stand for? **David**

2. Who became known as the man without a country? **Philip Nolan**

3. Who is the record holder for the most patents given to an individual? **Thomas Edison**

4. For what was Marie Curie awarded a Nobel Prize? **radioactive elements**

5. After Rosa Parks refused to give up her seat on the bus, who organized a bus boycott? **Dr. Martin Luther King, Jr.**

6. Who was the first woman pictured on a U.S. Postage stamp? **Martha Washington**

7. What does the "S" in Harry S. Truman stand for? **Nothing—he has no middle name**

8. Who is Cassius Clay? **Muhammad Ali**

9. Who was responsible for the voice of the early Mickey Mouse? **Walt Disney, Mickey's creator**

10. Louis Armstrong invented a singing technique known as scat. What is it? **It is singing without words, using nonsense syllables**

1. What man was a Nobel Prize winner, physical culturist, naval historian, biographer, essayist, paleontologist, taxidermist, ornithologist, field naturalist, conservationist, big game hunter, editor, critic, rancher, orator, country squire, civil service reformer, socialite, arts patron, cavalry colonel, former governor of New York, expert on big game mammals, and a U. S. President?

2. Before becoming aviators, Orville and Wilbur Wright were involved in what occupation?

3. How old was Winston Churchill when he entered Parliament?

4. What were Einstein's first three publications?

5. For what is Ricky Henderson best known?

6. For what is Arthur Ashe famous?

7. What hardship did Wilma Rudolph overcome?

8. Who was Anne of Cleves?

9. For what were Watson and Crick best known?

10. What kind of student was General George S. Patton when he was at West Point?

1. What man was a Nobel Prize winner, physical culturist, naval historian, biographer, essayist, paleontologist, taxidermist, ornithologist, field naturalist, conservationist, big game hunter, editor, critic, rancher, orator, country squire, civil service reformer, socialite, arts patron, cavalry colonel, former governor of New York, expert on big game mammals, and a U. S. President? **Teddy Roosevelt**

2. Before becoming aviators, Orville and Wilbur Wright were involved in what occupation? **Bicycle mechanics**

3. How old was Winston Churchill when he entered Parliament? **26**

4. What were the subjects of Einstein's first three publications? **Theory of relativity, the microscopic motion of molecules in liquid, and that light travels in waves**

5. For what is Ricky Henderson best known? **Stealing bases**

6. For what is Arthur Ashe famous? **First African-American to win a championship in tennis**

7. What hardship did Wilma Rudolph overcome? **Wore a leg brace as a child but won 3 gold medals in track and field in 1960**

8. Who was Anne of Cleves? **4th wife of Henry the VIIIth**

9. For what were Watson and Crick best known? **DNA**

10. What kind of student was General George S. Patton when he was at West Point? **He was not an outstanding student and took 5 years to graduate.**

How to play: Read each clue carefully. Research the biography of each suspect, finding out the one which comes closes to meeting the description. Circle that one.

1. This suspect was a classical musician who was internationally famous. He studied in Berlin and later came to America, becoming a citizen in 1941. He lived a long life and was in his 90s when he died. Was it Leonard Bernstein, Arthur Rubenstein, or Lucian Pavarotti?

2. This suspect was a famous architect who was especially good at math and physics. He studied at Oxford and later taught there. He rebuilt 52 churches destroyed by fire and was knighted by the queen. Was it William of Sens, Charles Rennie Mackintosh, or Christopher Wren?

3. This suspect was a philosopher and a successful doctor but is best known for his writings. He believed that faith and reason would lead to truth, an unpopular belief among his contemporaries. Was it Averroes, Avicenna, Diogenes, or Empedocles?

4. This suspect was an English biologist who was distressed about the outbreaks of smallpox and the 10,000+ deaths that resulted in England alone. He became rich by discovering a vaccine for this deadly disease and received a huge payoff from Parliament. Was it Charles Best, Francis Crick, William Harvey, Edward Jenner, or Joseph Liste?

5. This suspect was a sports star who came from a poor family. She participated in the Olympics and won seven Olympic medals. She died in 1938 at age 39. Was it Fanny Blankers-Koen, Dawn Fraser, Sonja Henie, Suzanne Lenghen, or Irena Szewinska?

6. This suspect was an American actor, director, and Academy Award winner. Although he directed films, he is best known for a still-famous radio broadcast produced during the 1930s. He died in 1985, the year of the crime. Was it Charles Chaplin, Samuel Goldwyn, Cecil B. DeMille, or Orson Welles?

7. This suspect was a famous Spanish-born painter who has had numerous fradulent reproductions of his work for sale on the black market. His work was outlandish, often bizarre. He has influenced the world of film, fashion, and advertising. He was born in 1904 and died in 1989. Was it Salvador Dali, Pablo Picasso, or Andy Warhol?

8. This suspect was a social reformer who was greatly concerned about poor women and the problems they faced. She began her work in Liverpool, where she founded the "Great Crusade" to protect poor women. Was it Annie Besant, Josephine Butler, Elizabeth Fry, or Marie Stopes?

9. Now: From the final list of suspects, select one who was European, lived in the 1900s, started out poor, rose to fame, and could have committed the crime in 1985. Who dunnit?

1. This suspect was a classical musician who was internationally famous. He studied in Berlin and later came to America, becoming a citizen in 1941. He lived a long life and was in his 90s when he died. Was it Leonard Bernstein, Arthur Rubenstein, or Lucian Pavarotti? **Arthur Rubenstein**

2. This suspect was a famous architect who was especially good at math and physics. He studied at Oxford and later taught there. He rebuilt 52 churches destroyed by fire and was knighted by the queen. Was it William of Sens, Charles Rennie Mackintosh, or Christopher Wren? **Christopher Wren**

3. This suspect was a philosopher and a successful doctor but is best known for his writings. He believed that faith and reason would lead to truth, an unpopular belief among his contemporaries. Was it Averroes, Avicenna, Diogenes, or Empedocles? **Avicenna**

4. This suspect was an English biologist who was distressed about the outbreaks of smallpox and the 10,000+ deaths that resulted in England alone. He became rich by discovering a vaccine for this deadly disease and received a huge payoff from Parliament. Was it Charles Best, Francis Crick, William Harvey, Edward Jenner, or Joseph Liste? **Joseph Liste**

5. This suspect was a sports star who came from a poor family. She participated in the Olympics and won seven Olympic medals. She died in 1938 at age 39. Was it Fanny Blankers-Koen, Dawn Fraser, Sonja Henie, Suzanne Lenghen, or Irena Szewinska? **Suzanne Lenghen**

6. This suspect was an American actor, director, and Academy Award winner. Although he directed films, he is best known for a still-famous radio broadcast produced during the 1930s. He died in 1985, the year of the crime. Was it Charles Chaplin, Samuel Goldwyn, Cecil B. DeMille, or Orson Welles? **Orson Welles**

7. This suspect was a famous Spanish-born painter who has had numerous fradulent reproductions of his work for sale on the black market. His work was outlandish, often bizarre. He has influenced the world of film, fashion, and advertising. He was born in 1904 and died in 1989. Was it Salvador Dali, Pablo Picasso, or Andy Warhol? **Salvador Dali**

8. This suspect was a social reformer who was greatly concerned about poor women and the problems they faced. She began her work in Liverpool, where she founded the "Great Crusade" to protect poor women. Was it Annie Besant, Josephine Butler, Elizabeth Fry, or Marie Stopes? **Josephine Butler**

9. Now: From the final list of suspects, select one who was European, lived in the 1900s, started out poor, rose to fame, and could have committed the crime in 1985. Who dunnit? **Salvador Dali**

1. James Earl Jones played the voice of Darth Vader in the "Star Wars" movies. For what else is he known? Do you think a particularly strong performance such as this one tends to stereotype an actor forever? Explain your answer.

2. Bonnie and Clyde made a ruthless pair of robbers during the Great Depression. What were their full names, what crimes did they commit, and why do you think Clyde earned the title of "public enemy number one"?

3. What were some of the jobs held by Wild Bill Hickok? What was his reputation? What do you think earned him the title "Wild Bill"? Give examples to support your answer.

4. Joseph Stalin's name was a pseudonym—Stalin meant "man of steel." Do you think this pseudonym fit? What other characteristics describe Stalin, in your opinion?

5. What influence do you think Karl Marx had on Lenin? Why do you think Lenin changed his name? How would you characterize this man?

6. Jack Nicholson played a number of evil characters in films such as *The Shining, The Witches of Eastwick, Batman*, and *Wolf*. Do you think an actor has to be evil to play an evil part so well? Explain your answer.

7. Richard Nixon was the only U.S. President in history to resign office. From the beginning, Nixon's political career was surrounded by controversy from bitter political battles, name-calling, misappropriating campaign funds, Vietnam and, finally, Watergate. Do you think all presidents are corrupt and Nixon was just unlucky enough to get caught or do you think he was unusual? Justify your answer.

8. Rasputin was a character of questionable background, but won over the Czar and Czarina through his "miracle healing" of their hemophiliac son. Do you think he was truly a miracle healer? Explain your answer.

1. James Earl Jones played the voice of Darth Vader in the "Star Wars" movies. For what else is he known? Do you think a particularly strong performance such as this one tends to stereotype an actor forever? Explain your answer. **Some acceptable answers are: he is the voice of CNN; he has appeared in Field of Dreams; and lent his voice to The Lion King. Accept all supported arguments.**

2. Bonnie and Clyde made a ruthless pair of robbers during the Great Depression. What were their full names, what crimes did they commit, and why do you think Clyde earned the title of "public enemy number one"? **Answers may vary, but all answers should reflect research into this couple, including full names and short history of crimes (list may vary as to what is included) as well as a strong reason for the title "public enemy number one."**

3. What were some of the jobs held by Wild Bill Hickok? What was his reputation? What do you think earned him the title "Wild Bill"? Give examples to support your answer. **Accept all supported answers that give evidence of research.**

4. Joseph Stalin's name was a pseudonym—Stalin meant "man of steel." Do you think this pseudonym fit? What other characteristics describe Stalin, in your opinion? **While subjective, the answer should reflect thought and research into both pseudonyms, Stalin, Stalinism, and so on.**

5. What influence do you think Karl Marx had on Lenin? Why do you think Lenin changed his name? How would you characterize this man? **Accept all supported answers.**

6. Jack Nicholson played a number of evil characters in films such as The Shining, The Witches of Eastwick, Batman, and Wolf. Do you think an actor has to be evil to play an evil part so well? Explain your answer. **Accept all supported answers. Look for examples from Nicholson's work in the answer.**

7. Richard Nixon was the only US President in history to resign office. From the beginning, Nixon's political career was surrounded by controversy from bitter political battles, name-calling, misappropriating campaign funds, Vietnam and, finally, Watergate. Do you think all presidents are corrupt and Nixon was just unlucky enough to get caught or do you think he was unusual? Justify your answer. **Accept all supported answers.**

8. Rasputin was a character of questionable background, but won over the Czar and Czarina through his "miracle healing" of their hemophiliac son. Do you think he was truly a miracle healer? Explain your answer. **Answer should reflect research into the time frame and political setting of the period as well as hemophilia, and Rasputin himself.**

Resources for Preparing Your Own InfoQuest Biography Program:

Boughton, Simon. (1988). *Great Lives*. Hong Kong: Grisewood and Dempsey, Ltd.

Herstory: Women Who Changed the World. (1995). NY: Viking.

Moss, Joyce and George Wilson. (1996). *Profiles in World History: Significant Events and the People Who Shaped Them.* NY: Gale Research.

Turner, Glennette Tilley. (1989). *Take a Walk in Their Shoes:* Biographies of 14 outstanding African-Americans-with skits about each to act out. NY: Puffin.

Turner, Glennette Tilley. (1997). *Follow in Their Footsteps:* Biographies of ten Outstanding African-Americans with skis about each one to act out. NY: Cobblehill/Dutton.

Chapter *16*

Assessing Your InfoQuest Program

Now that you are ready to implement your own *InfoQuest* program, you should also begin preparing to evaluate your success. More and more these days, school systems, school administrators, parents and the general public are calling for accountability in education. School library media specialists are not exempt. While it is important to provide evidence that your school library media center is well-stocked, well-staffed, and well-used, it it quite another to verify exactly how it is being used and by whom.

> **"Evaluation must be an ongoing process."**
> – *Doris Epler (1999, p. 296).*

My own experience with *InfoQuest* led me to develop some new tools for assessment. Initially, I measured the success of the program with figures showing the increase in student patronage, the increase in the number of teachers scheduling media center activities, the degree of improvement in parental involvement, and the amount of additional funding that was provided to continue the program. You must measure what is important to you in your situation. Your needs may be significantly different from mine or anyone else's. But facts and figures speak louder than generalities. Keep accurate records of the criteria you do measure and invite your co-workers, parents, and administration to review them. Your success will speak for itself.

General Suggestions

Some general suggestions on promoting your program which will also advertise your success are:

1. Keep track of student participation and announce it on a regular basis at faculty meetings, in the newsletter, on your web page, or over the intercom. You might even approach a local radio or television station. The radio stations, in particular, seem to love trivia questions. The disk jockey might even be willing to announce some of your questions on the radio.

2. Be visible at Open House, Parents' Night, Conference Day, and other after-school functions to share the success of your program. Have sample questions and other materials available to show. I kept my weekly questions in a laminated flip book with one question printed in large letters on each page. For special occasions, I laid out a display with the book flipped open to one question, a supply of pencils and answer sheets, and resource materials to help locate the answer on a table. I also kept sample prizes and awards and a chart showing participation by class or grade level. When appropriate, I mentioned the needs we had in continuing the program so that funding might be obtained.

3. Take photos and create a display for special occasions. Be prepared to share some of the questions and answers with interested parents and members of the community. Make sure that the display is portable and durable and can go outside the school to meetings, fairs. This is a great way to promote your program as well as publicize your needs within the community, particularly with organizations which are willing to support promising educational programs in the local schools.

Ways to Track Your Progress

There are several paths to choose from in accounting for your *InfoQuest* program. One path is to track your progress by grade levels, recording their courses of study, your collaboration with the grade level teachers or coordinators in those areas, and their scheduled activities in the school library media center. Another path is to measure separate classes and their success rates. Record projects by class, noting resources used, special need and comments to take into account in future planning. Your subject-specific information literacy skills as listed in Chapters 9–15 are useful in this initiative. A third path is to track individual students and individual skills. The skills continuum listed in Chapter 3 is useful here—measuring specific information literacy skills and noting progressive attainment of higher levels of skills from the onset of the program. Examples of all of these means of assessment as well as some additional assessment tools are included in this chapter.

It is up to you as a school library media specialist or classroom teacher to determine which means of assessment is appropriate for your situation. Some of these assessment tools may need slight revision in order to accommodate your needs. But there can be no doubt that your record-keeping is crucial to your role as a media specialist or classroom teacher. Budgetary needs and priority items for the upcoming year can be supported by the records you keep now. Services offered and evidence of additional clerical, paraprofessional, or other help can be determined from these records. Student achievement and resources used can be figured statistically for future planning. Evaluation of your performance on the job and even administrative support for continuing your program can come from these tools when properly used. Moreover, your assessment tools can support your collaborative work with the classroom teachers in evaluating their students.

Grade Level Assessment Form

The form below is a sample form made with the information literacy skills associated with science research as identified in Chapter 12. Similar forms can be created from the information literacy skills identified in each chapter. These forms can be utilized by the school library media specialist for use in collaborative projects in special subject areas by grade level. For example, an eighth grade science class may be working on a unit on chemical elements. The school library media specialist can track grade level activities on chemical elements by completing the form below. This form can be used year after year to assist in grade level planning meetings when preparing for the units of study covered during the course of the year. The form might also serve as a reminder of supplemental resource materials for inclusion in the budget and yearly planning process. Some modification may be necessary to accommodate the adaptations made in individual schools and local situations.

| **Figure 16.1** | *Information Literacy Project Assessment in Science Research* |

Grade Level _____ Instructor _____ Date _____

This class has achieved the following through research projects and assignments in the school library media center:

Description of assignment:

Grade level coordinator's duties:

School Library Media Specialist's duties:

Supplemental Materials used:

Resources obtained through interlibrary loan or outside sources:

Additional materials which might have been helpful in this project:

Information Literacy skills associated with this project:

- Restating a question in one's own words
- Identifying the keyword
- Formulating a list of related topics
- Recognizing sources that fit specific search criteria
- Testing a theory
- Devising a philosophy based on personal beliefs supported with research
- Using an index, table of contents, headings, subheadings
- Paraphrasing information
- Comparing information from various sources
- Summarizing information
- Writing notes
- Outlining
- Narrowing or broadening a topic
- Using charts, graphs, tables to organize and present information
- Identifying irrelevant statements
- Distinguishing between fact and opinion
- Retelling information in one's own words
- Creating a newscast, speech, documentary, or other form of presentation

Class Assessment Chart

The following chart is a sample form created specifically for use with individual classes which work as a group in the school library media center. The media specialist, in collaboration with the classroom teacher, works out a project timetable. The teacher schedules time periods in the media center and the media specialist locates and makes available resources and activities to support completion of the project. Recordkeeping such as the following form can assist both the classroom teacher and the media specialist in improving the project for the next class, anticipating and preparing for student pitfalls, and determining resource materials needs for the future. Such recordkeeping can also prove invaluable in demonstrating to the administration the need for inclusion of specific materials in the budget or planning for additional clerical or paraprofessional help.

Class _____ Grade Level _____
Instructor _____ Date _____

Description Of Activity: _____

_____

Objective: _____

Resources Utilized: _____

Information Literacy Skills: _____

_____

_____

_____

_____

Time Frame: _____

Description of Student Performance: _____

_____

_____

Goals Achieved: _____

_____

Areas which need improvement or additional work: _____

_____

_____

_____

Comments: _____

_____

Individual Student Assesment Forms

The following forms are designed for use with individual students, either by the school library media specialist or the classroom teacher, or both. These forms provide a more detailed accounting of student activities and achievements and may be placed in a student portfolio or student record folders to travel with the student from year to year. As with the other forms, some modifications and adjustments to suit your individual situation may be necessary.

It might work well to place a cardstock copy of the cumulative reference resource checklist form in an individual student folder and update it as the student progresses in his or her work with reference resources. Another suggestion is to make photocopies of the information literacy skills checklists on all four levels and place those into individual student folders as well. As the student progresses in information literacy skill levels, the forms provide a reference for growth from the onset of the student's participation in the program. Worksheets and copies of research projects might also be placed in this folder for perusal by parents during annual conferences, for teachers as student progress to the next grade level, for administrators when student placement is being considered, and in the cases of high school students, for guidance counselors to consider when assisting students with preparation of college essays and placement packages.

Figure 16.3 *Cumulative Reference Resource Checklist*

Student _____ Class _____

Check the months in which the student has had experience with the following reference tools in the school library media center.

	Aug	Sept	Oct	Nov	Dec	Jan	Feb	Mar	Apr	May	June
Atlas											
Almanac											
Anthology											
Bibliography											
Chronology											
Collective Biog.											
Dictionary											
Special Sub. Dict.											
Encyclopedia											
Special Sub. Enc.											
Gazeteer											
Index											
Thesaurus											
Yearbook											
Other											

Indicate any other reference tools with which the student has had experience, including electronic resources, the Internet, audiovisual resources and nonprint versions of the above reference tools.

Comments: _____

_____

_____

The following checklist is a compilation of the four InfoQuest Steps and corresponding information literacy skills on the preliminary level. Unlike the skills continuum in Chapter 3, related skills have been grouped together for efficiency of evaluation.

Figure 16.4 | *Preliminary Level* **Information Literacy Skills Checklist on** _____

The items checked below have been satisfactorily achieved through activities accomplished in the school library media center.

Inquiring

- ■ realizes that the library media center is a source of information, the library media specialist is a source of information, other individuals are a source of information
- ■ shows pleasure in visiting the library media center in supervised groups, in unsupervised groups, and individually
- ■ demonstrates responsibility in use of library media center materials
- ■ knows how to correctly handle books, magazines, and newspapers
- ■ knows correct procedure for borrowing and returning a book
- ■ can identify favorite author, illustrator, book character(s), story, series
- ■ can summarize favorite story
- ■ can describe favorite character
- ■ can communicate what she wants to know

Searching

- ■ recognizes that catalog provides information about title and author
- ■ realizes that the library media center houses a variety of materials and that materials in library media center are organized for easy access
- ■ can identify location of fiction books and nonfiction books
- ■ correctly identifies title, author, subject of a book
- ■ demonstrates knowledge of Dewey Decimal system
- ■ can put books in order by first number, first and second number, three or more numbers
- ■ can alphabetize by one letter, two letters, three or more letters
- ■ locates word in simple dictionary
- ■ locates word and meaning in a simple dictionary
- ■ can demonstrate use of a book to locate information
- ■ recognizes different types of books

Figure 16.4 *Preliminary Level (cont.)*

- knows location of different types of books in library media center
- uses dictionary to locate a word
- can identify the name of a source
- can locate a subject in an encyclopedia
- can use a mouse to point and click, open and close, manipulate desktop icons

Organizing

- can tell a teacher or media specialist what he has learned
- can state findings in own words
- can put events in proper order
- can use a storyboard to sequence story
- can select a format for presenting ideas: can draw a picture, make a simple chart, draw a short timeline of events, summarize important details
- can compose a title for a story, picture, or chart
- distinguishes between "real" and "pretend"
- gains information through listening or watching for a purpose

Sharing

- can demonstrate reaction to story by creating a picture
- can give a speech in front of the class
- clearly presents information learned
- presents information learned in sequence
- utilizes charts, graphs, and pictures to illustrate points
- notes location of information learned
- can show others how to locate same information
- can retell information in order in own words

The following checklist is a compilation of the four InfoQuest Steps and corresponding information literacy skills on the beginner level. Unlike the skills continuum in Chapter 3, related skills have been grouped together for efficiency of evaluation.

Figure 16.5   *Beginner Level* **Information Literacy Skills Checklist on _____**

The items checked below have been satisfactorily achieved through activities accomplished in the school library media center

Inquiring

- ■ can locate different types of resources with guidance.
- ■ can brainstorm for related ideas to a subject
- ■ can arrange books in order by one decimal, two decimals, three or more decimals

Searching

- ■ can identify subject headings
- ■ can identify subheadings
- ■ can skim or scan for information
- ■ reads captions for information
- ■ can use a table of contents
- ■ can use an index
- ■ can give the main idea of story
- ■ can identify the subject of a magazine article
- ■ use a thesaurus to locate a synonym or antonym
- ■ can use an almanac to locate a statistic
- ■ can use an atlas to find map information
- ■ can use a compass rose for orientation on a map
- ■ can interpret a map key
- ■ can interpret information from a chart, graph, table, picture
- ■ in a dictionary, locates word origin, locates part of speech, uses guide words, uses entry words, uses root words, uses context clues to select the appropriate meaning

Organizing

- ■ determines how to best share information learned
- ■ orally retells key points learned
- ■ participates in a group discussion on material learned
- ■ prepare a newscast, speech, or narrate a documentary audiotape
- ■ integrates multimedia and Internet sources into a presentation
- ■ writes information learned in own words in editorial, newsletter, report,

---

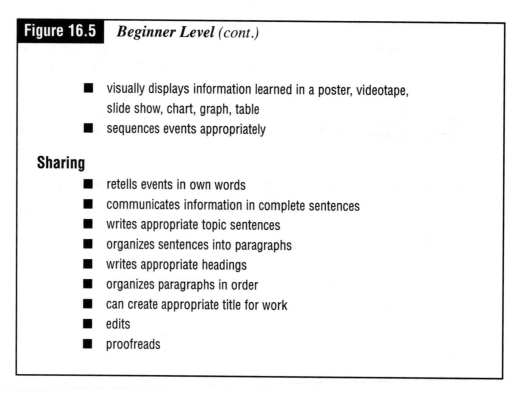

Figure 16.5 *Beginner Level (cont.)*

- ■ visually displays information learned in a poster, videotape, slide show, chart, graph, table
- ■ sequences events appropriately

Sharing

- ■ retells events in own words
- ■ communicates information in complete sentences
- ■ writes appropriate topic sentences
- ■ organizes sentences into paragraphs
- ■ writes appropriate headings
- ■ organizes paragraphs in order
- ■ can create appropriate title for work
- ■ edits
- ■ proofreads

The following checklist is a compilation of the four InfoQuest Steps and corresponding information literacy skills on the intermediate level. Unlike the skills continuum in Chapter 3, related skills have been grouped together for efficiency of evaluation.

Figure 16.6 *Intermediate Level* **Information Literacy Skills Checklist on** _____

The items checked below have been satisfactorily achieved through activities accomplished in the school library media center.

Inquiring

- realizes that print and nonprint sources serve different functions, that the same source can vary in print and nonprint formats, that sources of information can be primary or secondary, and that the best sources of information fit specific criteria
- visits the library media center frequently for both pleasure and research purposes
- visits the library media center for sources other than electronic media
- feels comfortable in the library media center either working independently or with a group

Searching

- knows correct procedure for placing a book on reserve or placing a hold on a book
- can identify call numbers for fiction
- can identify call numbers for non-fiction
- can identify a classic American literature title
- can identify a classic American literature author
- can refine question (broaden or narrow)
- can relate what is known to what is desired to be known
- can brainstorm a list of possible sources of information
- recognizes that a catalog provides information about illustrator, publisher, copyright date
- can identify the location of reference books, periodicals, computer software, audiovisual resources, catalog to locate resources
- can relate original idea to similar ideas for searching
- uses titles to determine if subject matter is suitable
- uses subtitles, subheadings to determine if subject matter is suitable
- compares information from various sources

Figure 16.6　*Intermediate Level (cont.)*

- in a dictionary uses pronunciation key, syllabication and accent marks, tenses, parts of speech, word origins
- uses keywords as a search strategy
- uses see and see also references in an index or catalog
- uses Boolean search strategy
- can summarize information found in a chart, graph, or table
- can determine distance using a map scale
- can demonstrate use of different types of maps (political, physical, contour)
- after viewing a videotape, can identify supporting details
- after listening to an audiotape, can identify supporting details

Organizing

- can organize thoughts in a web
- can write notes on main ideas located in a resource
- can use notes to organize information into an outline of reference material
- can outline and use notes to write paragraph in own words
- can proofread for omissions, insertions, indentions, tense, and other errors
- selects materials of appropriate length to complete a project
- can use a computer to organize files into folders, back up, create a shortcut, find files,
- resize windows, get help, use keyboard shortcuts
- can utilize database programs, spreadsheet programs, multimedia programs
- can perform an electronic search using Boolean search strategies, using quotation marks and parentheses
- can demonstrate careful use of peripherals (printers, scanners, cameras)
- convert files into multimedia format
- recognizes bias
- can identify irrelevant statements
- can skim/scan for information
- recognizes criteria for evaluation: currency, authority, validity, and so forth.
- can judge suitability of a resource for project
- can utilize note cards to organize search results
- can correctly compile bibliographical information
- can correctly compile citations
- can quote correctly
- can paraphrase correctly

Figure 16.6 *Intermediate Level (cont.)*

- can summarize and credit author correctly
- can utilize word processing tools to organize information gathered, specifically format with columns, with tabs, indent paragraphs, create headers and footers, and create master page for document
- can utilize spreadsheets to organize facts and data gathered, to create a chart or graphs, to format a key for chart or graph, and label axis for chart or graph
- distinguishes between fact and opinion
- correctly identifies different types of writing: narrative, persuasive, and so forth.
- can utilize databases to organize facts and data gathered
- can utilize databases to organize bibliographical information
- can correctly prepare a timeline, graph, chart, or table
- determines appropriate format for presentation
- determines appropriate mode of oral or written presentation: descriptive, narrative, persuasive
- if appropriate, effectively uses literary devices in presentation: dialogue, figurative language, foreshadowing
- supports all points made with effective, authoritative statistics

Sharing

- creates original visual aids to display information
- composes introduction
- composes conclusion
- correctly formats bibliography
- can correctly write footnotes, citations, and references in MLA or APA style, if necessary
- can create and maintain a web page to share information

The following checklist is a compilation of the four InfoQuest Steps and corresponding information literacy skills on the advanced level. Unlike the skills continuum in Chapter 3, related skills have been grouped together for efficiency of evaluation.

Figure 16.7   *Advanced Level* **Information Literacy Skills Checklist on** _____

The items checked below have been satisfactorily achieved through activities accomplished in the school library media center.

Inquiring

■ realizes that criteria can help in selection of appropriate sources, that related sources can provide additional sources of information, and that sources that provide related but inappropriate information should be discarded

■ uses time purposefully in library media center without supervision

■ demonstrates pleasure reading, browsing, and utilizing electronic resources and other media

Searching

■ knows correct procedure for searching other library catalogs and databases, ordering materials through an interlibrary loan

■ can identify location of classic world literature titles, authors, publication periods, genres (poetry, plays, literature, essays)

■ can formulate a research question, related themes or ideas, a theory to test, philosophy based on personal beliefs to support with research

■ recognizes that the catalog provides information to help locate a source, bibliographical information, and related resources on a topic

■ can locate resources using either the Dewey or LC cataloging format.

■ can narrow or broaden a topic

■ can determine specific criteria to fit topic researched.

■ uses a variety of reference tools including gazeteers, chronologies, indices, and more

■ uses collective and individual biographies for reference purposes

■ uses a variety of reference tools on a single research endeavor and knows the purpose of each

■ can use media such as video and audio players and tapes to gain information

---

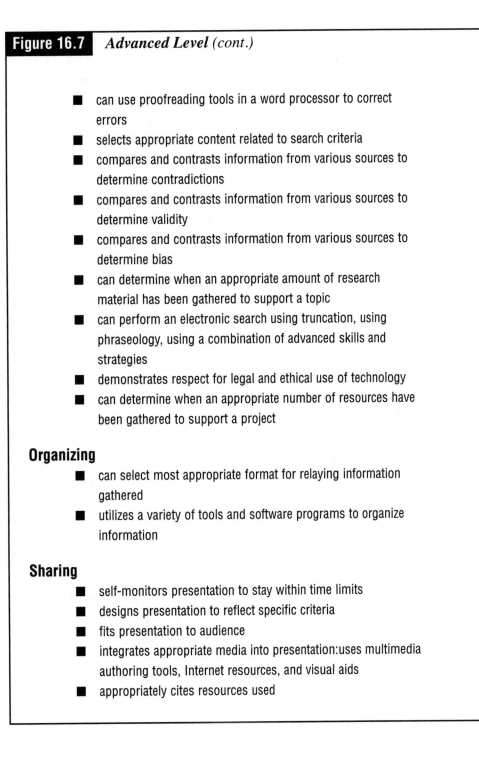

Figure 16.7 *Advanced Level (cont.)*

- can use proofreading tools in a word processor to correct errors
- selects appropriate content related to search criteria
- compares and contrasts information from various sources to determine contradictions
- compares and contrasts information from various sources to determine validity
- compares and contrasts information from various sources to determine bias
- can determine when an appropriate amount of research material has been gathered to support a topic
- can perform an electronic search using truncation, using phraseology, using a combination of advanced skills and strategies
- demonstrates respect for legal and ethical use of technology
- can determine when an appropriate number of resources have been gathered to support a project

Organizing

- can select most appropriate format for relaying information gathered
- utilizes a variety of tools and software programs to organize information

Sharing

- self-monitors presentation to stay within time limits
- designs presentation to reflect specific criteria
- fits presentation to audience
- integrates appropriate media into presentation:uses multimedia authoring tools, Internet resources, and visual aids
- appropriately cites resources used

Specific information is a necessity for citizenship in our society. All aspects of daily life are affected by the flow of data—industry, transportation, finance, housing, communication, entertainment, medicine, education, law, and more are information-driven. It is no longer enough for one to desire knowledge; the individual today must also possess the skills to access it. The ability to locate potential sources of information, retrieve the information, analyze the data found, and then utilize it effectively is known as information literacy.

InfoQuest is a program designed to help students develop information literacy skills. It works with children's natural curiosity and motivates them to learn more. Students work through four S.T.A.I.R.S (Steps In Achieving Independent Research Skills): Inquiring, Searching, Organizing, and Sharing. These steps are divided into clusters of skills on four levels: Preliminary, Beginner, Intermediate, Advanced. The program is designed to appeal to educators, media specialists, school boards, curricula committees, colleges of education, home schoolers, and more and has application in grades K-12.

The key to success in developing an *InfoQuest* program is in designing H.O.T. questions; that is, questions based on higher-order thinking skills. With specific adaptations to individual situations, an *InfoQuest* program is customizable for every student, classroom, subject area, school, or system.

InfoQuest can be used to raise funds, attract new patrons, and reinforce teacher-media specialist collaboration. Programs can be based on general reference work or specific subject areas. Because the specific skills associated with the program are measurable, and because the results measuring student progress in those skills can validate staffing, funding, curricula issues, and administrative support, assessment tools are critical. A variety of assessment tools are provided in this chapter.

Each and every student who becomes a regular participant in an *InfoQuest* program should come to the realization that specific information exists in specific resources, that specific skills are required to retrieve, organize, and communicate the findings, and that doing so is intrinsically satisfying.

References

Akin, Lynn. (1998). Information Overload and Children: a survey of Texas elementary school students. *School Library Media Quarterly*. Retrieved 5-12-01 from the World Wide Web site www.ala.org/aasl/SLMQ/overload.html

American Association of School Librarians and Association for Educational Communications and Technology. (1988). *Information power: building partnerships for learning*. Chicago: ALA.

American Library Association. (1995) Presidential committee on information literacy: final report. Chicago: ALA. Retreived January 2 ,1999 from the World Wide Web site: gopher://ala1.ala.org:70/00/alagophiv/50417007.document

American Library Association. American Association of School Libraries. (1996) Position statement on information literacy. Chicago: ALA adopted from the Wisconsin Educational Media Association. Retrieved May 10, 2000 from the World Wide Web site:http:// www.ala.org/aasl/positions/ps_infolit.html

Applebury, James B. (August 28, 1992). Remarks made in a speech on information literacy presented at California State University, Long Beach, California. Retrieved June 4 2000 from the World Wide Web site http://www.ala.org.acrl/nili.html

Association of College and Research Libraries. (March, 1998). A progress report on information literacy: an update on the American Library Association Presidential Committee on information literacy: final report. Retrieved 2/10/01 from the World Wide Web site: www.ala.org/acrl/nili.nili.html

Association of College and Research Libraries. (2000). Information literacy competency standards for higher education. Chicago: American Library Association. Retrieved May 11, 2000 from the World Wide Web site: http:// www.ala.org/acrl/ilintro.html

Association for Supervision and Curriculum Development. See ALA's Presidential committee on information literacy.

Association for Teacher-Librarianship in Canada and the Canadian School Library Association. (1999). Students' information literacy needs: competencies for teacher-librarians in the twenty-first century. *Foundations for effective school library media programs*. Englewood, CO: Libraries Unlimited, pp. 89-94.

Bailey, Gerald D. and Dan Lumley (1999) Fishing the Net. *Electronic School*. January, 1999. Retrieved July 31, 2000 from the World Wide Web site http://electronic-school.com/199901/01/199f4.html

(Bartlett's Familiar Quotations, 1992, p. 355)

Bloom, Benjamin. (1956).*Taxonomy of educational objectives: Handbook I cognitive and affective domain*. New York: David McKay Company, pp. 201-207.

The Boyer Commission on Educating Undergraduates in the Research University. (.(1998)). *Reinventing undergraduate education: a blueprint for America's research universities,* p. 6. Retrieved 8/7/00 from the World Wide Web site: www.uidaho.edu/~mbolin/doherty.htm

Bradbury, Ray Douglas. (1976). *Writers' digest,* February, 1976, p. 25.

Carvin, Andy. (Sept 30, 1999). Technology professional development for teachers: overcoming a pedagogical digital divide. *The digital beat.* V1 no. 16. p. 2. Retrieved 10/1/99 from a post to the LM_NET listserv.

De Cervantes, Miguel. (1615). *Don Quixote,* Book III, Chapter 6, p. 479.

Churchill, Sir Winston. (1992). *Bartlett's Quotations,* 16th Edition. New York: Little, Brown, and Company, p. 629.

Clemons, Samuel. (1992). *Bartlett's Quotations,* 16th Edition. New York: Little, Brown, and Company, p. 528.

The Clinton-Gore Administration. (April 4, 2000). A national call to close the digital divide. Office of the Press Secretary, the White House, Washington, D.C. Retrieved 6/4/00 from the World Wide Web site: www.webzone.net/machadospage/fact_sheet_on_closing_the_digital_divide.html

Davis, Barbara Gross. (1999) Motivating students. Tools for teaching. Berkeley, University of California. Retrieved 10/8/00 from the World Wide Web site: http://uga.berkeley.edu/sled/bgd/motivate.html

Doiron, Ray. (1999). Curriculum encounters of the third kind: Teachers and teacher-librarians exploring curriculum potential. *Foundations for effective school library media programs.* Englewood, Co: Libraries Unlimited.

Donnelley, Kimberley (2000). Reflections on what happens when librarians become teachers. *Computers in libraries* Vo. 20, No. 3, March 2000. Retrieved 8/17/00 from the World Wide Web site www.infotoday.com/cilmag/mar00/ donnelly.htm

Dowling, Susan. (July 8, 1996). Collaboration: The key to the process. Speech made at the National Conference of the American Library Association, The President's Council. Retrieved September 21, 1999 from the World Wide Web site: http://anansi.panix.com/~goldfarb/libpow/collabor.htm

Doyle, Christina. (1999). Information literacy in an information society. *Foundations for effective school library media programs.* Englewood, CO: Libraries Unlimited, pp. 97-100.

Epler, Doris. (1999). From library program to learning resources program: cooperative program planning and teaching. *Foundations for effective school library media programs.* Englewood, CO: Libraries Unlimited, p. 216.

Eisenberg, Michael B. and Doug Johnson. (March, 1996). Computer skills for information problem-solving: Learning and teaching technology in context. ERIC Clearinghouse on Information & Technology. EDO-IR-96-04. Retrieved 7/28/00 from the World Wide Web site: http://askeric/org/ithome/digests/ compterskills.html

Facione, Peter A. (1996). Critical thinking: what it is and why it counts. Millbrae, CA: California Academic Press. Retrieved 8/13/00 from the World Wide Web site: www.calpress.com/critical.html

Fromm, Eric. (1992). *Escape from freedom,* Chapter one as cited in *Bartlett's Quotations,* 16th Edition. New York: Little, Brown, and Company, p. 704.

Gordon, Julie. (1996). Tracks for learning: metacognition and learning technologies. *Australian Journal of Educational Technology,* Vol 12, No. 1, pp. 46-55. Retrieved 9/17/00 from the World Wide Web site: wwwasu.murdoch.edu/au/genaset/ajet/ajet12/wi96p46.html

Greenspan, Alan. (July 11, 2000.) Structural change in the new economy, a speech made to the National Governors' Association 92nd annual meeting, State College, PA. Retrieved July 28, 2000 from the World Wide Web site: http://www.federalreserve.gov/ BoardDocs/Speeches/2000/20000711.htm

Hancock, Vicki. (May, 1993). Information literacy for lifelong learning. Syracuse, NY: ERIC Digests #ED358870. Retrieved May 10, 2000 from the World Wide Web site: http://www.ed.gov/databases/ERIC-Digests/ed358870.html

Haycock, Ken. (2000). What works: applying research in information literacy. *Teacher Librarian.* Retrieved June 2, 2000 from the World Wide Web site: www.teacherlibrarian.com/whatworks27,3.html

Hepworth, Mark. (1999). A Study of undergraduate information literacy skills: the inclusion of information literacy and skills in the undergraduate curriculum. 65th IFLA Council and General Conference, Bangkok, Thailand. Retrieved 8/7/00 from the World Wide Web site: www.ifla.org/IV/ifla65/papers/107-124e.htm

Higher Education Council. (July, 1997). *Quality in resource based learning: Executive Summary.* Retrieved May 1, 2000 from the World Wide Web site: http://www.detya.gov.au/nbeet/publications/hec/rbl/rbl.htm

IFLANET (1999). Quotations about libraries and librarians: Subject List. Retrieved 7/26/00 from the World Wide Web site www.ifla.org/I/humour/subj.htm

King, A. (1994). Inquiry as a tool in critical thinking. *Changing college classrooms: new teaching and learning strategies for an increasingly complex world.* San Francisco, CA: Jossey-Bass Publishers, p. 13.

Kranich, Nancy. (December, 2000). A message from ALA President Nancy Kranich. *American Libraries.* Vol. 31, No. 11, p. 5.

Kuhlthau, Carol C. (Fall, 1993). Implementing a process approach to information skills: a study identifying indicators of success in library media programs. *School Library Media Quarterly,* vol. 22, no. 1, pp. 11-18.

Lance, Keith Curry, Marcia J. Rodney, and Christine Hamilton-Pennell. (1999). *Information empowered: the school librarian as an agent of academic achievement in Alaska schools*. Juneau: Alaska State Library.

Lance, Keith Curry, Marcia J. Rodney, and Christine Hamilton-Pennell. (2000). *Measuring up to standards: the impact of school library programs and information literacy in pennsylvania schools*. Camp Hill, PA: Pennsylvania Citizens for Better Libraries.

Lance, Keith Curry, Marcia J. Rodney, and Christine Hamilton-Pennell. (2000). *How school libraries help kids achieve standards*. Castle Rock, CO: Hi Willow Research and Publishing.

Leibovich, Lori. (August 10, 2000). Choosing quick hits over the card catalog. *New York Times*. Retrieved 8/10/00 from the World Wide Web site: www.nytimes.com/library/tech/00/08/circuits/articles/10thin.html

Loertscher, David. (1999) All that glitters may not be gold. *Foundations for effective school library media programs*. Englewood, CO: Libraries Unlimited, pp. 147-151.

Loertscher, David V. and Blanche Woolls. (1997). The information literacy movement of the school library media field: a preliminary summary of the research. CSU School of Library and Information Science. Retrieved 7/26/00 from the World Wide Web site: http://witloof.sjsu.edu/courses/250.loertscher/modelloer.html

Lubans, John. (September, 1999). When students hit the surf. *School library journal online*. Retrieved 8/25/00 from the World Wide Web site: http://206.236.152.83/articles/articles/19990901_6516.asp

Lyle, G. R. (1963). The president, the professor, and the college library. New York: H.W. Wilson as cited in the case for information studies. Retrieved 8/6/00 from the World Wide Web site: www.accd.edu/pac/lrc/iscase.htm

Marland, Michael. (1999). Libraries, learning and the whole school. *Foundations for Effective School Library Media Programs*. Englewood, CO: Libraries Unlimited, pp. 48-54.

McKenzie, Jamie. (September, 1996). Framing essential questions. *From now on,* Vol. 6, No. 1, September, 1996. Retrieved 8/31/00 from the World Wide Web site: Http://www.fno.org/sept96/questions.html

McKenzie, Jamie. (March, 1997). "Deep thinking and deep reading in an age of info-glut, info-garbage, info-glitz and info-glimmer." *From now on*, Vol. 6, No. 6. Retrieved 8/31/00 from the World Wide Web site http://questioning.org/Q5/ deep.html

McKenzie, Jamie. (October, 1997)."The question is the answer." *From now on,* Vol 7, No. 2. Retrieved 8/31/00 from the World Wide Web site http://questioning.org/Q6/question.html

McKenzie, Jamie. (1999). The research cycle. *From now on,* The educational technology journal. Vol. 9, No. 4, December, 1999. Retrieved September 30, 2000 from the World Wide Web site: http://questioning.org/recycle.html

McKenzie, Jamie. (September, 2000). Beyond edutainment and technotainment. *From now on,* The educational technology journal. Vol 10, No. 1, p. 5. Retrieved September 26, 2000 from the World Wide Web site: http://fno.org/sept00/eliterate.html

Marland, Michael (1999) Foundations for effective school library media programs. Englewood, CO: Libraries Unlimited, p. 54

Milken Family Foundation. See Solmon, Lewis C.

Miller, Marilyn L. and Dr. Marilyn L. Shontz. (October 1, 1999). How do you measure up? School library journal online. Retrieved 9/17/00 from the World Wide Web site: www.alj.com/articles/articles/19991991_6686.asp

Murray, Hubert, Jr. (March 8, 1966.)*Methods for satisfying the needs of the scientist and the engineer for scientific and technical communication* in a press release, Washington, D.C. as quoted by Mark R. Nelson.

Naisbitt, John. (1982). *Megatrends: ten new directions transforming our lives*. NY: Warner Books, Inc., p. 24.

National Council on Educational Statistics (1999). See Rowand, Cassandra.

Nelson, Mark R. (2000) We have the information you want, but getting it will cost you: being held hostage by information overload, ACM crossroads student magazine, pp.1-9. Retrieved July 31, 2000 from the World Wide Web site: http://www.acm/crossroads/xrds1-1/mnelson.html

Nock, Albert Jay. (1992). *Bartlett's Quotations*, 16th Edition. New York: Little, Brown, and Company, p. 610.

Oberg, Antoinette. (1999). The school librarian and the classroom teacher: partners in curriculum planning. *Foundations for effective school library media programs*. Englewood, CO: Libraries, Unlimited, pp. 167-174.

Orr, Debbie, Jacqueline Slee and Efthimia Evryniadis. (1999) International students and the electronic library facilities at Central Queensland University. Strategies for the next millenium: Proceedings of the ninth Australasian information online and on disc conference and exhibition. Sydney, Australia. Retrieved 5/5/01 from the World Wide Web site: http://www.csu.edu/au/special/online99/ proceedings99/304a.htm

Page, Carol-Ann. (1999) Collaborative planning: a model that works. *Foundations for effective school library media programs*. Englewood, CO: Libraries Unlimited, pp. 189-204.

Page, Carol-Ann. (1999) Information skills in the curriculum: developing a *school-based curriculum*. Foundations for effective school library media programs. Englewood, CO: Libraries Unlimited, pp. 122-129.

Pitts, Judy M. (Spring, 1995) edited by John H. McGregor and Barbara K. Stripling. Mental models of information: the 1993-1994 AASL/Highsmith Research Award Study, *School Library Media Quarterly,* vol. 23, no. 3, p. 177-184.

Pound, Ezra. (1992). *Bartlett's quotations,* 16th Edition. New York: Little, Brown, and Company, p. 660.

Rankin, Virginia. (1999). *The thoughtful researcher: teaching the research process to middle school students*. Englewood, CO: Libraries Unlimited, Inc. and its Division: Teacher Ideas Press.

Risko, Victoria J., Marino Alvarez, and Marilyn M. Fairbanks. (1991). Teaching reading and study strategies at the college level. Newark, Delaware: International Reading Association as cited in "The Case for Information Studies." Retrieved 8/6/00 from the World Wide Web site: www.accd.edu/pac/lrc/iscase.htm

Routh, Martin Joseph. (1992). *Bartlett's Quotations*, 16th Edition. New York: Little, Brown, and Company, p. 355.

Rowand, Cassandra and the National Center for Educational Statistics. (1999). Survey on public school teachers use of computers and the internet conducted through NCES fast response survey system. Retrieved 5/10/00 from the World Wide Web site: http//nces.ed.gov

Simmons, Rebecca. (1994). The horse before the cart: assessing for understanding. *Educational leadership,* Vol. 51, No. 5, February, 1994, p. 1. Retrieved 5/10/01 from the World Wide Web site: www.ascd.org/readingroom/edlead/9402/simmons.html

Small, Ruth V. (1999). An exploration of motivational strategies used by library media specialists during library and information skills instruction. School library media research. Retrieved 5/12/01 from World Wide Web site: www.ala.org/aasl/SLMR/vol2/motive.html

Small, Ruth V. (1998) Designing motivation into library and information skills instruction. School library media quarterly. Retrieved 5-12-01 from the World Wide Web site www.ala.org/aasl/SLMQ/small.html

Snyder, Timothy. (1998). Librarians are still keepers of the flame. *Pueblo chieftan,* April 19. Retrieved 6/2/00 from the World Wide Web site: http://monte.k12.co.us/admin/librarian2.htm

Solmon, Lewis C. and Judith A. Wiederhorn. (2000). Milken Family Foundation's progress of technology in the schools: Report on 27 States. Retrieved 5-12-01 from World Wide Web site: www.mff.org/publications/publications.taf?page=282

Southern Association of Colleges and Schools, (December, 1996). *Criteria for accreditation*. 10th ed. as listed on the World Wide Web site: http://www.sacs.org/pub/coc/cri70.htm and retrieved May 10, 2000 from the World Wide Web site: http://www.cas.usf.edu/lis/il/definitions.html

Starr, Linda. (1999) Growing bigger brains: research affects how teachers teach. *Education World*. Retrieved June 2, 2000 from the World Wide Web site: www.education-world.com/a_curr/curr140.shtml

State University of New York Council of Library Directors. (1997) *Information literacy initiative*. *Final report*. New York. Retrieved May 10, 2000 from the World Wide Web site: http://www.sunyconnect.suny.edu/ili/final.htm

Straathof, Sharon. (1999) Developing a school-based research strategy K-7. *Foundations for effective school library media programs*. Englewood, CO: Libraries Unlimited, p. 139.

Swanson, Troy A. (2000). They're the DJs, we're the rappers. *American Libraries*. March, 2000, Vol. 31, No. 3, pp. 32-33.

Tarasof, Mary and Sonya Emperingham. (1999). From library program to learning resources program: cooperative program planning and teaching. Foundations for effective school library media programs. Englewood, Co: Libraries Unlimited, pp. 215-222.

Tomlinson, Carol Ann. (2000). Reconcilable differences: standards-based teaching and differentiation. *Educational leadership,* Vol. 58, No. 1, September, pp. 5-11.

De Unamuno, Miguel. (1992). *Bartlett's Quotations*, 16th Edition. New York: Little, Brown, and Company, p. 589.

Usiskin, Zalman. (1993). Lessons from the Chicago mathematics project. *Educational leadership,* Vol. 50, No. 8, May, 1993. Retrieved 5/9/01 from the World Wide Web site: www.ascd/org/readingroom/edlead/9305/usiskin.html

U.S. Department of Commerce's National Telecommunications and Information Administration. (July, 1999). Falling through the net: Part II—Internet access and usage. Retrieved 7/28/00 from the World Wide Web site: www.ntia.doc.gov/ntiahome/fttn99/part2.html.

U.S. Department of Commerce's National Telecommunications and Information Administration. "Falling through the net: Part III— defining the digital divide. Retrieved 7/28/00 from the World Wide Web site: http://www.ntia.doc.gov/ntiahome/digitaldivide/factsheets/access.htm.

U.S. Department of Education (1999). National Center for Education Statistics (NCES) See Rowand, Cassandra.

Valenza, Joyce Kasman. (1996). Information literacy is more than computer literacy. *School crossings,* Retrieved 8/7/00 from the World Wide Web site: http://crossings.phillynews.com/archive/k12/infolit4_16.htm

Warmkessel, M.M. and McCade, J.M. (1999). Integrating information literacy into the curriculum. *Research strategies*. Vol 15, no. 2, pp. 80-88.

Whetzel. Deborah. (1990). U.S. Department of Labor Secretary's Commission on Achieving Necessary Skills (SCANS) Report. Washington, D.C. Retrieved May 10, 2000 from the ERIC Digest World Wide Web site: http://www.ed.gov/databases/ERIC-Digests/ed339749.html

Wurman, Richard Saul. (1989). Information anxiety. New York: Doubleday.

Name and Topical Index